KU-256-988

MONOLOGUES

FOR

WOMEN

BY

WOMEN

WITHDRAWN

LIVERPOOL JMU LIBRARY

3 1111 01072 6873

LIVERPOOL JOHN MOORES UNIVERSITY
Aldham Robarts L.R.C.
TEL. 051 231 3701/3634

WITHDRAWN

LIVERPOOL JOHN MOORES UNIVERSITY
Aldham Robarts L.R.C.
TEL. 051 231 3701/3634

MONOLOGUES

FOR

WOMEN

BY

WOMEN

EDITED BY TORI HARING-SMITH

HEINEMANN
Portsmouth, NH

Heinemann
A division of Reed Elsevier Inc.
361 Hanover Street, Portsmouth, NH 03801-3912
Offices and agents throughout the world

Copyright © 1994 by Heinemann.

Every effort has been made to contact the copyright holders for permission to reprint borrowed material where necessary. We regret any
oversight that may have occurred and would be happy to rectify them
in future printings of this work.

All rights reserved. Except for brief passages quoted in a newspaper,
magazine, radio, or television review, no part of this book may be
reproduced in any form, or by any means, electronic or mechanical,
including photocopying and recording, or by an information storage
and retrieval system without permission in writing from the authors.

Performance rights information will be found at the end of this book.

Library of Congress Cataloging-in-Publication Data
Monologues for women, by women / edited by Tori Haring-Smith.
      p.   cm.
   Includes index.
   ISBN 0-435-08630-8 (alk. paper)
   1. Monologues. 2. Acting. 3. American drama—20th century.
4. Women—Drama. I. Haring-Smith, Tori.
PN2080.M538 1994
812'.04508—dc20   94-1259
                                                    CIP

Interior design by Tom Allen, Pear Graphic Design

Printed in the United States of America on acid-free paper
03 02 01   EB   8 7

Contents

Subject Index

The Feminist Movement and Individual Revolutionary Acts

Identity

Lesbian Love

Marriage and Other Long-Term Relationships

Bagshaw-Reasoner, Tough Love
Carpenter, The Ride
Lipkin, Excerpt from *Small Domestic Acts*
Martin, For Better or Worse
Miller, Nasty Rumors and Final Remarks
Monroe, Alabama Red Dirt
Moraga, Excerpt from *Giving Up the Ghost*
Sheehan, Bright Girls, Stupid Lives
Simpson, Equal Unto the Angels
Vogel, Desdemona
Weaver, Momma's Little Helper

Mother/Daughter Relationships

Bingham, In the Presence
Bock, Suicide Note
Browde, Temporary Shelter
Cohen, Philomela's Tapestry
Goldenthal, Birthday
Mueller, Florence Commuter Airlines
Neipris, Separations
Overmyer, Emily
Weaver, Momma's Little Helper

Pregnancy, Abortion, and Motherhood

Danticat, Rose
Kelly, Loreli
Magee, Blue
Miller, Flux
Neipris, Separations
Silberman, Antlers on the Wall
Spector, Another Paradise
Zohn, Joan

Race and Class

Sex and Sexuality

The Silenced Woman

Violence and Rape

Introduction

Why a Collection of Monologues for Women, by Women?

THIS COLLECTION OF MONOLOGUES for women, by women, gives actresses an opportunity to present themselves through the words and visions of other women. The characters who speak in these pieces are women as they are understood by other women. These writers know what it is like to grow up female, to encounter the world through female eyes. This is not to say all women understand one another, or that there is a universal female experience. The experience of a black heterosexual is necessarily quite different from that of a white lesbian or an Asian bisexual. Privileged women lead very different lives from unprivileged ones. Our views of life change as we go from twenty to forty to sixty, and as we pass from daughter to mother, or from partner to loner. And even these broad categories are deceiving since, above all, we are all individuals. This collection gives voice to fifty of these unique female visions.

The authors represented here are students, professional playwrights, actresses, mothers, businesswomen, teachers, producers, directors, and retirees. They are black, white, Asian, Hispanic, wealthy, poor, urban, rural, lesbian, heterosexual, and bisexual. Some of them are angry, some scared, some amused, some loving, some timid, some raging. They have drawn pictures of women pilots, bag ladies, Greek heroines, bakery workers, mothers, daughters, travellers, battered wives, civil rights advocates, tap dancers, and anthropologists.

If there is no universal female experience, then what makes these characters different from the much more numerous female characters drawn by male writers? Unfortunately, no matter how sympathetic, well-read, or empathic male writers may be, they can only understand the female experience as outsiders. Even those men who think they have suffered as women have suffered are misled. Being a battered wife is different from being a battered male child. The female rape survivor has a different story than the male rape survivor, because the male and female are allowed such different kinds of power in our society. And a quick glance at female comics like Kathy and Mo reveals how different female comedy is from male. This is not to say that men are incapable of understanding women or that they purposely misrepresent them. But inevitably, most men write women through the lens of their own experience. For years, women's lives have been shaped by the patriarchal culture and the literature of that culture. Women's voices, their stories, have been silenced, or ignored. The authors who created these monologues have done what most women yearn to do—they have crafted and defined their female lives.

Within this collection, "women's issues" do not stop with the traditionally female topics like abortion, domestic violence, rape, unequal pay, menopause, dieting, and birth. The women who speak on these pages also talk about fishing, soldiering, physics, advertising, and Shakespeare. Some of these women say things "women don't say" in polite company. When women take the right to speak, women may just as easily talk about clitorises or lynchings as about tea parties. Thus, this collection expands the category of "female concerns."

I also hope that some of the monologues demonstrate the artificiality of the category "women's issues." Why should subjects like abortion and domestic violence be pigeonholed as "women's issues"—as if they have nothing to do with men? Aren't these problems the symptom of larger social ills that touch all human beings? Even personal subjects such as menstruation and menopause are as much a part of society's life as military history and male infidelity. Until we recognize the centrality of female lives to our entire society, producers and artistic directors will continue to sideline our experiences, fearing to stage more than one "women's play" (if that many) in a given season. The more we can demonstrate the importance of "women's issues" to our entire society, the more likely that someday powerful people in theatre will worry about doing too many "men's plays." Remember that most theatre tickets are purchased by women, and that there are more females than males in the major actors' unions. Clearly women are attracted to the theatre as practitioners and consumers— yet their stories are woefully underrepresented, except in the rare environment of a "women's" or "feminist" theatre company.

Because women's work is so rarely staged, it is also rarely published, making it difficult for female actors and directors to find. As a result, when I audition women, I watch one after another belittling herself or shaping herself to accommodate a man's vision. As I coach actresses, they often say, "But I don't understand this woman; I would never react that way!" And usually, their "problem" is that they are being asked to enact male fantasies of the female experience. This inability to understand and enact male visions of female experience is what can earn women the labels "insane" and "hysterical."

This collection gives women a chance to speak the words of other women. And it adds to the growing awareness of women playwrights. Some of these monologues are designed to be part of one-woman shows. Others were written as audition pieces or excerpted from longer works. You will find biographies of each of these writers, and also contact addresses, so that you may write them about their work. This collection is one more step toward answering the question, "Where are the women playwrights?" They are everywhere. Just listen.

Tips on Auditioning with a Monologue

Choosing a Monologue

In order to perform a monologue well, you should have some personal connection to it. You need to understand the character's emotion, and be passionate about her concerns. After all, you are going to have to explore this character in depth and then generate enough energy to make her live for your audience. In some cases, actors are drawn to monologue characters because they have undergone similar experiences. If the character is talking about death, and you have recently lost a loved one, you may be able to share something of yourself—your grief—in bringing the character to life. Remember, acting is about sharing yourself. That's one reason why actors must learn to be vulnerable, and yet to relax. When you audition, your audience wants to know who you are, as well as who you can be. Your choice of a monologue often reveals you, so choose carefully.

It is common advice that monologues should talk about the present, not just recount the past. I think this advice, while well-intentioned, is artificially limiting. There is nothing wrong with a monologue that tells a story from the past as long as you, the actor, make it present and active. As long as the story is a vital part of the character you develop, it will stir emotions, shape interactions, and reveal layers within the character. Remember that all monologues have at least one silent stage partner, someone who is listening and responding to the character, perhaps driving the character to keep speaking. Sometimes the silent partner is another character, sometimes another facet of the speaker, and sometimes the theatre audience. As long as the monologue connects with your passions, you will be able to make it live for your silent stage partner, and for your audience.

Even though a monologue springs from the interaction of two characters, it must not be too dependent on the context of the play if it is going to stand on its own in an audition. That is, the monologue needs to make sense and be important in its own right—not just because of its function within the play. Many of the most exciting monologues in full plays simply cannot stand on their own, because in isolation they do not reveal the character fully enough. Most successful audition monologues do not refer to too many people other than the speaker. It's difficult to keep track of a woman's lover, husband, daughter, and business associate in the course of one two-minute monologue! The primary purpose of a monologue is to showcase you, not the play or the playwright. A monologue should require no more introduction or explanation than the title of the play.

It is important that a monologue (or pair of monologues, if you are performing two together) allow you to show a range of emotional, physical, and vocal qualities. While you can get some range by choosing a pair of contrasting monologues, each piece you do should have some variety within it. The emotional state of the character needs to be dynamic, so that you can show more than one side of your emotional, physical, and vocal life. If you are choosing a pair of monologues, you will probably want to find speeches of different subjects as well as with differing tones.

When choosing a monologue, try to find material that will be new to your audience. When I audition large numbers of people, I frequently hear the same monologues over and over again. I have to force myself to listen to painfully familiar pieces like the twirler from *In the Boom Boom Room*. When you choose a classical monologue, think about how many Juliets or Kates your auditioners will have heard on the professional stage and in auditions. Try to find some new material. Women playwrights from the Middle Ages, Renaissance, Restoration, and Eighteenth Century are just now being rediscovered and published. Look for collections of their work, and you may find wonderful new monologues. Although this collection will not help you find a classical monologue, it will provide you with fifty previously unpublished or hard-to-find contemporary pieces.

Finally, be sure the monologue is suitable for you, and for the theatre or film you are auditioning for. This does not mean the character has to match you identically in race, gender, age, or geographical location. Just be sure that you understand the character and how she responds to life. If you feel that you would respond as she does, you probably have a sympathetic relationship to the character. If you are playing someone much older or younger than yourself, do not "play age"—play yourself. Avoid pieces that require a strong accent unless you are told that you need to demonstrate particular dialect abilities.

Think about the suitability of the monologue for the medium in which you are auditioning. If you are being seen for television work, the monologue should be "PG" rated. If you have been called for a particular role, try to find a monologue that is stylistically linked to that script or role (i.e., use a comic piece if you're auditioning for a comedy) but is not from the script itself. The auditioners will have all kinds of preconceived notions about the roles they are casting. If you pull a monologue from the play they have been dreaming about for several months, you may not seem right to them if your interpretation of the character does not match their ideal for it. If the auditioners want to see you in the part, they will ask for a cold reading.

Finally, think about the length of your monologues. Do not cram so much into your two or three minutes that you feel rushed while you are performing. Respect the time limits set by the auditioners. Some of the monologues in this book are obviously too long to be done in an audition. In those cases, you can easily extract a two- or three-minute audition piece from the longer selection. Having the entire monologue not only gives you context, but also gives you material for longer performances in showcases and workshops.

Preparing and Rehearsing
As you rehearse your monologue, either alone or with a coach, use the techniques that have been most successful for

you in preparing full-length roles. If the piece is from a longer work, read the play. But do not rely on the longer work to "explain" the character—your auditioners may not know the piece. The monologue must stand on its own as a comprehensible piece, telling the auditioners all they need to know about your characters. Also, don't let the full play's context limit you. Don't assume that because the character in the play is insane, your interpretation of the monologue must also reveal insanity.

More important than any research in the library, more important even than reading the full script is careful examination of the specific text you are going to present. Think about the character drawn there, and ask yourself the usual character development questions, such as:

- Who is this person talking to? Does that shift at any point during the piece? What does the listener want from the speaker?
- What question or event is the speaker responding to? What happened just before she began to speak?
- What does the speaker need? Why does she keep on speaking? (Make this need as important as possible.)
- What are the conflicts within the speaker, and between the speaker and her listener(s)?
- What does the speaker's language reveal about her? What is the speaker's favorite word in this monologue?
- How is the speaker different after she has said her piece than before? What has she gained, lost, discovered?
- What line in the monologue is the most important? Where does the speech make emotional turns, and reach a climax?

As you explore the character, keep reassuring yourself: You are not looking for the "right" answers. You are looking for answers that are emotionally truthful, that you can play. Be faithful to your own experience and your own sense of truth—not to what someone else thinks that character "should" be like. Do not be satisfied with quick, easy answers. Keep probing.

As you work on the character, consider her vocal and physical life. Would she sit down, or is she too overwrought? Does she try to hide her strong emotions behind civilized, controlled speech, or does she speak out? Experiment with different actions you might give the character as well. Is she knitting while she talks? Fidgeting with a button? Putting on make-up? Consider her stance. Does she stand tall? Hunch forward? Sit primly? Be sure you make choices that allow you to keep your head up and that do not force you to move so frenetically that the auditioners cannot "see" you for the movement. Know where your silent partner is. Do not make the auditioner a silent partner—no one wants to be forced to participate in an actor's piece. Does the silent partner move at any point? Where, when, and why?

As you rehearse, concentrate on your primary goal of making your character present and active. Command attention—think of what Linda Loman says about Willy: "Attention must be paid." If you know what the character wants, you will have no trouble bringing that need out for the audience.

Once you begin to put your performance together, consider how you will start. You are, in fact, "on" from the moment you walk onto the stage. Practice introducing yourself pleasantly and efficiently:

Hello. My name is _____, and today I'll be doing monologues from Joan Lipkin's *Small Domestic Acts,* and Mary Pix's *The Innocent Mistress.*

Then work on the transition into your first monologue. Take a moment to visualize your character's situation, to ground yourself in her needs, to place your silent partner, and to think about the question or event you are responding to. Practice this kind of preparation, and you will not need more than five to ten seconds to accomplish it.

Work through the transitions between monologues in the same way. After you have chosen an order for your pieces, consider how you will move smoothly from one to the other. Be sure that you complete the first monologue, give it a beat to sink in, then alter your physical stance in some way and quickly launch into your second piece. As you rehearse, have someone time your work. When you are performing, you want to be able to think about the character, not the clock. Take your time to live the character fully but not self-indulgently. And, above all, don't be afraid of being boring. If you think you're boring, you're going to telegraph that to your auditioners, and your worst nightmare will come true.

Plan what you will wear to the audition. Think of something that complements your body type and doesn't distort your presentation of either of your characters. You do not want to look costumed during your audition; you want to look as much like yourself as you can. The goal of the audition is to reveal yourself and the range of your abilities. You may costume one character by adding or taking off a jacket or sweater, but do not plan elaborate costume changes. Most people do not change costume at all during their auditions. After all, you should be able to present the character without relying on a costume to support you. Similarly, you may need one small prop in one of your monologues—a pencil, a book. If you need more props than that, you have not chosen an appropriate audition piece. Remember that the only furniture you can count on having is a folding metal chair. Try to be as self-sufficient as possible, and not to rely on costumes, props, or furniture. Your acting, and not the technical aspects of your performance, must be the focus. Your auditioners should remember you, not your costume.

As you rehearse, keep exploring. Take risks; that's what rehearsals are for. If you find that you're afraid of looking foolish—playing either too big or too small—face your fears. Do the monologue as you fear it might be seen at its very worst. Facing your fears will make them dissolve. But if you don't face them and enact them, they will inhibit your spontaneity, and make you censor yourself. Sometimes, you will discover that your worst nightmare may have been an excellent choice for the piece—you were just afraid of taking the chance. Don't be afraid to be quirky or bold.

Some people hire coaches to help them prepare monologue work. Whether you rehearse alone or with a coach, at some point you need to practice performing your work in front of different audiences. Don't always practice or perform in the same studio. Move around. Get used to performing anywhere so that the strangeness of the audition situation will not throw you. If you can perform with equal concentration and comfort in a living room, on a stage, in a classroom, and out of doors, you're probably well prepared for your auditions.

Presenting Yourself and Your Work
Before your audition, try not to establish expectations. You should be aware of any rules that have been set for the audition—number of pieces you should present, your time limit, requirements for the types of monologues—but go into the audition without any expectations about the process itself. Don't "picture" the room, because you may be surprised, and then you'll have to deal with that surprise when you should be acting. If you think, "Oh, I'll be up on a big stage in a 2000-seat auditorium," and you end up auditioning in a hotel conference room, you'll have trouble making immediate adjustments, and doing so will distract you from concentrating on your monologue.

Don't even make assumptions about the behavior or number of people who will be watching you. Sometimes you will be performing for one person, sometimes for fifty or sixty in combined auditions such as Straw Hat, or Midwest Theatre Auditions. Don't anticipate rapt attention from your auditors. They may look at you intently, they may eat while you perform (we often don't get lunch breaks), or they may pass papers around or talk about you. Don't be surprised, don't be thrown. Just do your work and let them do theirs. It is hard not to be offended if someone is talking while you perform, but keep your concentration on your work. Remember, they may be saying, "She's perfect for the part, isn't she?"

Get a good night's sleep before your audition and wear comfortable clothes. If you're going on a callback, wear the same or similar clothes that you wore to the first audition. If the auditioners liked that person, they will remember and like the same person during callbacks. Wearing a T-shirt and jeans to the first audition and then a suit to the callbacks only confuses the people who are trying to find the real you. Bring extra copies of your picture and résumé in case you need them.

Know where you are going and give yourself plenty of time to get there. You may have forms to fill out, and you will want to warm up before your audition. Find a quiet place to center yourself, warm up vocally and physically, and run over your piece to be sure you are comfortable with it. If you can't find a private place, just close your eyes, focus, and take yourself through the piece in your head. Follow the emotional track of the character and visualize your silent partner. In other words, perform in your head. This is the same practice that professional athletes engage in when they visualize themselves making a free-throw or kicking a goal before they act.

When it is time for you to audition, you will be admitted into the audition room by a monitor or the casting director. In most cases, you or the casting director will have sent your picture and résumé to the director. If not, hand them to the director as you enter the room and cross to the audition area. If the director initiates a conversation, respond politely and efficiently. Think of this as a cocktail conversation. Most directors, though, will not initiate conversation. They're rushed and they just want to see who you are.

As soon as you enter that room, seize the space. Walk confidently and know that for the next three minutes, you are in charge of what happens. It is all too easy to experience auditions as a kind of meat market, in which you are just a number. In fact, auditions are often like this, but you must never present yourself as "just one more actor." Take the stage. Know you're important. If you need to move a chair or set up the space, do so quickly. Then pause to be sure that the director is ready for you to proceed. In some cases, a monitor will indicate when you should begin. Introduce yourself and your piece, making eye contact with the director or with as many of a large group of directors as possible. This is the only time during the formal part of the audition that you should make direct eye contact with the auditioners. Set up your space so that you are facing the auditioners, but put your silent partner to one side of them, or behind them. Once your introduction is over, take a few seconds (no more) to focus completely on your work, and then go.

At the end of the performance, wait a beat, break character, and then say, "Thank you." If, for some reason, the director wants to see more of you, you may be asked to do a cold reading or additional monologues. Always have some additional work in reserve. It is not uncommon, especially in graduate school auditions, for directors to request specific types of monologues. "Do you have something more upbeat?" "Do you have something in verse?" "Can you show us a more vulnerable character?" You can never be prepared for all requests, but have a supply of work at your beck and call. But if you are not asked to do additional work, don't be depressed. You may not have suited the role, or you may have been so perfect that the auditioners know immediately that they want to see you at callbacks.

When you've finished, never comment on your own work. Especially do not apologize. The most important thing is to be confident and to look like you're having a good time throughout the ordeal. Don't even comment on your own work by scowling, frowning, or shrugging as you walk away.

Once you have left the audition, try not to second guess the director. Even if the director seemed to respond well to your work, don't begin to fantasize about what it will be like to work with that director or on that project. If you don't get the part, you'll just be doubly disappointed. Every actor needs a strong support system. You put yourself on the line daily—you are the product that you are selling—and although you know that not everyone wants or needs your product, it is never easy to take rejection. Remember that even famous actors face rejection every day. Keeping faith in yourself and in those around you who stay by you in your times of need will see you through and keep you sane.

Auditioning can be a nightmare, but it can also be fun. You meet lots of different people, get tips on upcoming projects, and have a chance, however brief, to perform. Just keep reminding yourself that you are in control of your performance. No matter how good you are, you will only be right for some roles. Can you imagine Roseanne Arnold as a sensitive figure-skater? Keep true to your own sense of self, keep polishing your acting skills, and be sure that you have other ways of measuring your self-worth aside from getting cast in any one given role.

Tough Love

NANCY BAGSHAW-REASONER

(Paula is talking with her husband.)

PAULA: I wanted to go to Paris, when I was younger. I wanted to live in a garret and paint and drink wine. And make it with a different Frenchman every night. No ties. No possessions. Just my paints. A wine glass. Well, two wine glasses. I came close. I was a nude model for a figure drawing class, at NYU. Well, the money was incredible! I'm serious! For that time. The minimum wage was . . . what, $1.60 . . . and I got four or maybe it was five bucks. Of course, it was tough. You try sitting like this for an hour. (*She strikes a pose*) My hands and feet would go numb. Then my tailbone would go to sleep. They'd call a break and I'd jump up to grab my robe and I'd collapse in a heap. Of course, they were used to that. All the nude models staggered a lot. But they loved my bottom. And that made me feel so . . . unique . . . unconventional . . . daring. . . . Yes, that's it. Daring.

I went home for Christmas that year . . . to my parents' house. I'd been modelling since . . . oh, July? And we go to friends of Mother and Dad's . . . the Hughes. They're having this little dinner thing. And they say, "Bring Paula. We haven't seen her since she moved to New York." So we go and I'm telling everyone that I'm working in this Market Research firm. And I'm BSing like mad. And then we go into the dining room, and there, hanging over the buffet, lit for God's sake, is a huge oil nude. And, son of a gun, it's me! And I'm dying and everyone's admiring it and Mrs. Hughes is trilling about how they bought it at a student art show and isn't it sensuous and aren't they just on the cutting edge for patronizing young artists and nah . . . nah . . . nah. . . . And I wanted to say, "Guess what, fellow art lovers, that's me! That's my ass!" (*Pause*) But I didn't. (*Pause*) I didn't tell them because I wanted to fit in with them. I wanted to be like them. I wanted a risk-free life. (*Pause*) And that's why I married you.

Into the Fire

DEBORAH BALEY

(Rosie is talking to her neighbor Billy about her experiences while waiting for her husband, Hank, to come home. She lives in Alaska.)

ROSIE: I had to, Billy. It was my last chance. I was sittin' in that chair there—the one you're sittin' in now—the one I sit in every night when I wait for Hank to come home from the bar. I'd been sittin' there for hours. It was like I was dead. And I thought . . . I might as well be. (*Pause*) And then, one of the springs pushed up through the cushion into the back of my leg. It made me jump. I just . . . *jumped* . . . out of the chair. Next thing I know, I'm thrashin' around the room, the way a bear thrashes when it wakes in the spring. You know why bears thrash when they wake, Billy? So they know that they're *here*. So they know they're *alive*. Because after a sleep, they don't know. I woke up from a sleep. I didn't know where I was. (*Pause*) I caught myself in the mirror. It stopped me, dead in my tracks. I just stood there, lookin', for a long, long time. . . . I saw nothin', Billy. Nothin' at all. All I could see were my clothes—just a mound of gray wool with two eyes lookin' out. So I threw them off. I just stripped them right off. I looked at myself in the mirror. I'd never really looked at myself before. And I thought . . . what *is* this? This . . . *thing* . . . with two arms and two legs? This thing lookin' back with two vacant eyes? What *is* it? I didn't know. . . . It's a piece from an old puzzle, I thought . . . an old piece that had fallen, forgotten, under the couch. No, I thought. It's a . . . *star*. The first star that a young child draws. No, it's a. . . . (*Pause*) I didn't know! I ran out of the house to look up at the sky,

3

only there weren't any stars out, just the moon peekin' through from the clouds, and I thought . . . this *thing* . . . what is it . . . is it me? It's not a piece from a puzzle, or a child's first star . . . is it me? And then (*Pause*) . . . something happened in my body. I was standin' on the path in a mud puddle, and I looked up and saw the moon. Something came over me. I started to howl . . . the way a wolf howls when she's callin' her young back to the den. Next thing I know, the whole town is there, standin' around me. (*Pause*) Then, Hank stepped out of the crowd. He put me over his shoulder, took me back home and threw me in bed. (*Pause*) The whole thing feels like a dream. . . .

In the Presence

SALLIE BINGHAM

(Lou, an older white woman who was once famous for her active role in the civil rights movement, talks about her daughter, Martha, with occasional references to Ken, her husband.)

LOU: Martha spent almost two months in the detention center, from the time she was thirteen till she died. Oh, it was little things—running away from home, and they'd pick her up and take her on down, and I was being hard-assed, I'd tell them to keep her a while. I remember one time some matron down there tried to persuade me to take her home: "This isn't the right place for your daughter, Mrs. Alden." She didn't know me, she meant the black kids down there—always more black kids in any dump this society sets up, public school time-out rooms, juvenile detention centers, later on, jails. That made me so mad I swore I'd leave her down there a month, learn a lesson, maybe. But she never learned a thing. Just walked out of there when I finally came to get her with a big plastic smile, told the judge at every hearing and pretrial and trial that all she had was family problems—and of course those men were plenty willing to believe that, Mama not home fixing cookies but off trying to fix things in this sick society.

The last time she was in there, she wrote me a letter, scrawled it on a sheet of lined yellow paper, handed it to me at visiting time—black mothers and black sons, mostly, crowded around those long metal tables, trying not to cry, ending up laughing at nothing. Oh, I remember! Handed me that yellow paper, slipped it in my pocket so the guard

5

wouldn't see. Just a few lines—I read them in the car: "I don't want to live if I can't come home. Let me come home now, Mama, please." I said to Ken, "That's the biggest piece of manipulation yet"—you see, we'd been seeing a therapist, he said she was all the time manipulating us. "She'll be threatening suicide next," I said, and I wouldn't let her come home, I let the state give her a lawyer, go through a lot of hearings, decide she was illegally detained—she hadn't committed any crime, after all—and then, when they finally let her out, I gave her to the state and they took her to a group home. I got to the point, I was burning up, I couldn't think about anything but her lies, her pale little face and her big red lies. She knew what I wanted to hear: "I love you, Mama, I'll do everything right from now on, just the way you want it, you'll see." She knew how hungry I was to hear that! She practically wouldn't speak to Ken—knew he was on her side, already— and just concentrated all that LOVE on me. I hadn't had any love from that girl from the day she was born, and here she was, focusing it all on me like a bright hot light. But I KNEW it was a fake, I knew she didn't feel it, she was just working me over, the way a thief'll work over a zonked-out addict, seeing has he got some change in his pockets. Because she knew I was an addict, too, I needed her love, I never have been able to kick it.

Suicide Note

ELSIE ERVIN BOCK

(Beverly drinks alone as she contemplates suicide.)

BEVERLY: I can't be like Janine. You always wanted me to, and I can see why. But I'm not like that. I'm fat. Don't shake your head, Mama. I have looked at my naked body, and it's fat. Yes, Mama. I've taken your advice. I've tried dieting. In fact, I am the world's foremost authority on dieting. Just ask me anything. Let's see now. First, of course, I tried diet pills, back when they were the rage and back when I was popping other pills too. Then I tried the banana diet. Then I tried the banana and wienie diet, three bananas one meal and three wienies the next. That worked for a while, but you can only endure bananas and wienies so long. Then I tried the No-Carbohydrates diet, which worked wonderfully except that your sweat takes on this strange odor, and I decided I'd rather be fat than smell bad. I've tried the Cambridge diet, the grapefruit diet, the Dream-Away diet. ("Take two tablets on an empty stomach"—well, my god, who couldn't lose weight going to bed every night on an empty stomach!) Let's see now. There was the Fat-Burner diet and the Starch-Burner diet, and all the doctors' diets. Anyway, I'm still fat. My third therapist thinks people choose to be fat, to punish themselves. Who knows?

Janine. She was just like you. Pretty, and on the inside of things. You probably don't even know what that means, Mama, because sometimes when you're on the inside you don't even know there is an outside. But it's like this—the girls who dated in high school were on the inside. All the young people in church groups who go to youth fellowship meetings and summer camps—they're on the inside. No, that might not be true. It's only the ones who get chosen to be on a softball team, or get picked to bunk with the other girls. If you're one of the ones left over who has to be placed somewhere by a counselor, you are definitely not on the inside. "Oh, and here's Beverly. Let's see, Beverly, maybe we can put you in the cabin with. . . ." (*Pause*)

I can't deny any of it. I've read all the do-it-yourself psychology books. I have played all the games. (*Pause*) But Mama, I've learned things. I've learned there's no such thing as love. Oh, there's lust, there's desire. Mama, sometimes I'm so filled with plain ole animal desire that I would take any man who happened to be around. Well, hold it, now. Not any man. Don't count Alfred Wainwright. You always wanted to fix me up with Alfred Wainwright. He came from a "good" family. Just looking at him squelched any desire I ever had. (*Pause*) But don't you see, Mama, instead of loving a particular man, a person can just want to make love! I know that's foreign to you. But we fool ourselves. That's mostly what love is—self-deceit. Who do we really love but ourselves—our rotten, dishonest, fat selves. (*Drinks*)

Mama, I'm trying to be honest. Do you hear me? Honest. There's just no more pretending. I promise to quit committing suicide if you promise to stop drinking decaffeinated coffee. Or something like that. Is that a deal? We've got to face it, Mama. It's just us. You and me. And what do you think will happen to us? I'm really curious about that. In fact, I'm curious about a lot of things. I want to see how everything turns out. I want to see if it's going to rain tomorrow like the weatherman says—and if the Dodgers will win the World Series—and if what's-her-name sleeps with what's-his-name on *All My Children*. I want to see if Dr. Pittman-Shitman will sue me for not paying my bill!

I want to see if I turn into a fat old lady or a skinny old lady!—fat chance!—I want to see if this god-damned apartment building gets condemned next week!

No, Mama, I'm just too damn curious to commit suicide.

Temporary Shelter

BETH BROWDE

This piece was originally performed at the National Theatre in Washington, D.C.

My mom tried to drive me off a bridge once. I'm not kidding. The Triborough Bridge. She was in a really bad mood—really bad. She was taking me to the airport so I could visit my dad in Paris. The whole thing was her idea—I didn't want to go to Paris anyway, and I would've been happy to take the bus to the airport.

Now the truth is, I think she'd been mad at me for a while—basically since I was born. But some days we got along fine. Anyway, she's driving me to the airport and Grandpa is in the front seat. Now Grandpa was the best person I ever knew. He was nice to everyone no matter what. So she stops the car and says to him, Get out of the car. I'm going to kill her and I don't want you to get hurt. He doesn't really believe her. You don't mean that, dear, is what he says. But she insists she does mean it. She is going to kill me. And he gets out. 125th Street and Broadway.

Now, I don't think I thought she meant it, 'cause I just stayed there in the backseat and didn't say a word. At the time I thought silence was the most sophisticated approach— I mean, I was only eighteen. But whenever she started screaming at me, I would just shut up and look out the window. She hated that. I don't remember what she was saying. She always liked to discuss her impending divorce in the car.

One time on Highway 81, in the middle of Pennsylvania, she's yelling at me and my brother and she just stops the car—right in the middle lane. She doesn't pull over to the side at all. She says to my brother, I'm not going any further until you tell me who you would rather see dead—me or your father. Cars are whizzing by us, honking and pointing. My brother thinks the whole thing is pretty funny, and he says, If I promise to answer the question, will you drive? So she says yes and starts driving and he says, You. I'd rather see you dead.

The next day she tried to run him over with the car.

That's the main reason to keep my mouth shut.

That's what I did the whole time I was growing up—kept my mouth shut. There's a good and a bad side to it. The bad side is it can take you half an hour to find the bathroom in a strange place. But the good side is you don't say anything stupid, even if you're thinking it. If you keep your mouth shut long enough, someone's bound to give you a hint.

But sometimes I can't help talking. So probably I said something wrong. Anyway, there we were in the car driving across 125th Street. She's telling me about how I'm gonna get up in court and tell the truth about what a bastard my father is. And I'm thinking to myself, What's the point of being married to someone who doesn't want to be married to you? Then I make a mistake. I say it out loud. We're just about to Lenox Avenue and I say, Look, Mom, I don't understand. What's the point of being married to someone who doesn't want to be married to you? She starts screaming, floors it, and tries to drive the car right into the wall of this Kentucky Fried Chicken restaurant on the corner—turned into two lanes of oncoming traffic. So I dive headfirst from the backseat into the brake. Her legs are jerking all over the place. She is sort of spazzing out. Somehow we stop and I grab the keys, screaming my head off for help. The only thing is this: We're there in this giant Oldsmobile Nighty-Eight blocking an entire intersection in the middle of Harlem. She's wearing her mink coat and all this jewelry. All these people are crowding around the car. All these black people. And we look like two rich crazy ladies, and I think: I'm a liberal, but how are they going to know? And I'm afraid to open the door. I'm totally panicked. And all of a sudden my mom is completely calm. She says, Janice, give me the keys and I will drive you to the airport. That's it. Not please, not I'm sorry, just give me the keys. And you know what I did? I gave her the keys.

So she starts the car and we're going along, me in the front seat this time. We don't talk. I just look out the window. I don't even remember thinking—just blank. But pretty soon she's at it again, saying I should have a good time in Paris, because she'll be dead when I get back. And I say something really stupid, So, who's supposed to feed the dog while you're dead? I mean, I know it was a really stupid thing to say, but I guess I was pretty mad at her by then and I was thinking of the time before when she took fifty Seconals and left a note in the kitchen that said, While I'm dead, feed the dog.

By now we're on the bridge. She starts screaming that she is really going to kill me, and she turns sharp to the right across two lanes. I grab the wheel and try to jam on the brake, and we sort of bounce off this cement embankment. And I grab the keys again.

And the same thing happens again. I'm crying and screaming and she's completely out of control, yelling and spazzing out. Two lanes of traffic on the bridge are stopped and honking at us. Then all of a sudden she's fine, like nothing happened. She tells me to give her back the keys, she promises not to kill me, and so I do.

That seems really weird, doesn't it—me just giving her back the keys like that.

So it was about four years later that I went and found this shrink, Phyllis. She was nice. By then my mom had died. It was like, while she was alive, I didn't really want to talk about it too much. I mean, I guess I'm lucky she died so I could stop thinking I was the one who was crazy.

But one day I'm in there telling this shrink, Phyllis, about being driven off the bridge, and the time she tried to run my

LIVERPOOL JOHN MOORES UNIVERSITY
LEARNING SERVICES

brother over and the Seconals—all those stories. And Phyllis is listening real intently. And suddenly I think, oh my God. How is she gonna know I'm not just making this up? What if my mom is just this nice lady who bakes cookies and sends me presents? How would she know? Everything she knows about me is what I say. What if I'm lying? Or what if I don't even know that I'm lying, and I'm just deluded, and none of the stuff I remember actually happened?

So, anyway, here's what happened with my mom. She finally gets me to the airport. Nobody was dead, but I have to say I was probably the least excited person with a ticket to Paris at Kennedy Airport. I don't have the slightest idea what I said to her when I got there, but she stormed out, saying, Have a good time. I'll be dead when you get back. All right, I'm going to tell you something. At that point I wouldn't have minded if she was dead, but I just wasn't in the mood to go to Paris. I find out that there's a place in the basement of the airport where you can make an emergency transatlantic call. So I go down there and I find this Air France office, and I tell the guy it's an emergency, I have to call my father in Paris. Now, you would think, just by the way I looked—I was crying so hard I could hardly talk—you would think someone would just make the call. But this guy says he has to know why or he can't do it. So I tell him basically my mother has just tried to kill me on the way to the airport and just left saying she was going to kill herself. And I mention the Seconals so he knows she knows how to do it. So he gets the number of my dad's hotel and makes the call. But there's no answer.

So he says to me in his most sympathetic voice, You know, I'm a businessman, just like your father. And the most efficient way to handle this is for you to get on the plane, meet with him in Paris, and then if you want, take the next flight back. Then I understood. He didn't care about me or anything I was saying. He just wanted to sell plane tickets. He just wanted the fucking money.

I started to argue with him, when in walks my mother like she's on her way to a garden party, smiling and completely together. She says, I thought you'd be here. Come on dear, we don't want you to miss your plane.

Well, that guy just looked at me like I was out of my mind. So this must be your mother, he says. Your daughter and I were just having a little chat. He smiled at me.

Sidewalks

HEIDI CARLA

(Lone Woman addresses the audience in the manner of a stand-up comic or street commentator. She sports a beltpack and canteen. The action takes place on the street, not in a nightclub.)

LONE WOMAN: How are you all tonight? My god, there's enough of you. Ooooh . . . feel those vibes just rippling over me . . . *wow* . . . how do you do that? *(Long pause as she beams at the audience)*
 I'm thrilled to be a part of the exciting events this evening. I know that some of you have come from faraway and exotic places . . . like *Pittsburgh* and *Providence* to be here tonight. To come together in this very large recreation hall within this wonderfully generic cement building . . . behind the car park . . . in the worst section of the city. Was it just me . . . or did anybody else have trouble finding this place? Raise your hand if you did *(She raises her hand)*—c'mon, be honest. I see lots of lost expressions in this audience. Why are these functions always held in outlying areas? Nuclear reactor sites have been built closer to civilization. No, really, I didn't have too much trouble finding it 'cause I brought along my compass and my girl scout survival kit.*(She shakes her canteen.)* I still have enough water in here to last me a few days. I had only a few moments to peek at the roster outside the door . . . glanced over the names of the women that organized the events here this evening. All of them wonderful committed comrades. I won't mention your names . . . the list is too long. I go way back with some of you; old college chums like Harriet . . . oophs . . . sorry . . . sorry, *HOPI*

Smith. It's HOPI now . . . and Sioux Martin . . . that's S-I-O-U-X. Knew her when she was just plain "Sue." Ovilla Sandstone from Albany (*She directs a wave and wink at Ovilla in the audience*) and Azure Skye . . . ya know, anyone else would have walked away thinking they had stumbled onto an Indian Craft and Jewelry Convention by mistake. I just said—*whoa*, what's this . . . will I be the only *cowboy* here tonight?

No really . . . I'm all for reinventing identities. I changed my name and identity six times on the way over here tonight. SIX TIMES . . . and I can do it again . . . (*She snaps her fingers.*) quickquick . . . gimme a role model. (*She takes a drink.*) It's only *tea* . . . really. I know I should go easy on this stuff. It's a real problem with me because I consume a large amount of fluids and always have to relieve myself at inopportune moments . . . no matter where I go. I have to seek out restrooms in the seediest places sometimes. But don't worry about the restrooms here. I already checked them out . . . yeah . . . and I'm happy to report they're spanking clean. There's perfumed soap in those little push-up caddies and individual packets of hand lotion to prevent your hands from drying out and there's . . . get this . . . TWO restrooms . . . in case you didn't know, you have a choice: One has a sign says "*women*" and the other says "*womyn.*"

I stood there for a few minutes, trying to decide which door to walk through . . . and nearly peed my pants while deliberating. Seriously, I shouldn't complain 'cause I love to perform at feminist functions.

There's excitement in the air . . . you can feel all those positive electrons charging up the atmosphere . . . new ideas just bouncing off the walls. Everyone is so responsive and perky. Well, I'm a little suspicious about that perkiness, 'cause that may be attributed to all that caffeine we intake night after night, hanging out at those coffeehouses. We all know that coffee isn't good for us. We gotta find another place. Another *beverage*. Somewhere we can go to relax and talk. I toyed with the idea of opening a communal soup kitchen, but then you'd always be wiping broth dribble from your chin. May even start calling each other names like Charlie and Winnie. None of that *pueblo panorama* we have here this evening. Yes indeed . . . there is no question about it . . . coffeehouses have made us a proud race. I'll drink to that . . . tea . . . coffee . . . (*She takes a sip.*) I'll stick to tea right now . . . thankyouverymuch. (*Pause*)

There are more serious problems on the horizon than caffeine that I should address . . . but I won't . . . there isn't enough time in one evening. I have been preoccupied with problems of my own that I should air out. Problems that plague me personally as a performer. I'm always afraid of *misplacing* my sense of humor as a feminist. You know we women never actually *lose* anything. We just put it in a safer place and then forget where that is. But, it *almost* happened to me this morning. I woke up in a cold sweat and panicked. I absolutely couldn't think of one joke that wasn't sexist . . . racist . . . homophobic . . . capitalistic . . . related to drugs and alcohol . . . and non-vegetarian. It took *three cups of coffee* before I was politically correct. I'm telling you . . . It's a real concern for some feminists, to be politically correct all the time. I'm not from the "Miss Manners School of Comedy" myself, so you'll have to pardon me if I step on the toes of some unfortunate persecuted minority. Way I see it . . . is that I don't owe the Women's Movement too much courtesy since they never even bothered to give me a measly "pronoun" they have been promising for years.

The Ride

BRIDGET CARPENTER

(Alice, an elderly woman, talks to her dog, Sparky, recounting memories of her life with Frank, her husband.)

ALICE: I put some old hamburger in there tonight. (*She hands an imaginary bowl to Sparky, who takes it between his teeth and places it on the floor. He sniffs suspiciously. Alice speaks partially to herself.*) Hamburger was Frank's favorite meal. He never liked anything fancy. He could eat a hamburger every night. "Alice, you should start a chain like McDonald's," he would always say. He picked you out, you know. You were the scrawniest looking pup of Maddie McPherson's dog's litter. Frank just saw you and said, "I bet this one likes hamburger too, think so, Alice?" I said I thought so. And we took you home. By then Betsy had already grown up, and I wasn't in the wheelchair yet. Remember?

That was when we went on some great rides. (*Alice holds out her hand. Sparky does not see this, but he knows it is there, and he leaves his food to go to Alice and be petted. She pats him vigorously.*) When Frank didn't mind driving all day to get to a really good roller coaster. You loved those car rides. And those coasters! Such wonderful long rides . . . every coaster with an exciting name . . . the Phoenix. Hercules. Screaming Eagle. Le Mistral. Dragon Fyre. And Frank could never convince the operator to let you get on the coaster with us—even though he tried every time. "Let the dog have some fun!" he would shout. But you never got to ride. Just watched from the ground, barking to beat the band. You'd make such a fuss! And Frank would always yell at the ride operator after it was over. "You should have let the dog come!" he'd say. Oh, my.

And you were even worse after we joined the American Roller Coaster Enthusiasts' Club. All those parks where we were allowed Unlimited Ride Time . . . and we'd ride until we were dizzy . . . and the wind rushed past our ears as we flew through the air . . . the wind! Lifting us up, carrying us beyond earthly sadness or pain. Whshhh! Whshhh . . . whsh-hh . . . whshhh . . . (*She raises her arms slightly, as if on a coaster.*)

. . . And you'd just sit and bark. You were such a worried puppy, watching us go! The trip home, Frank would always sing, "When Irish Eyes Are Smiling. . . . " So sweet. So sweet-ly. And he'd always say, "If only the dog could've taken a ride with us." Mm-hmm. We've been together quite a while. (*He puts his paw on her knee with a heavy thud. They sit for a moment. Alice begins to sing tunelessly.*)
When Irish eyes are smiling
Oh it's like a summer day
But when Irish eyes are laughing
Oh it's like a big parade . . .

(*During this, Sparky has begun to howl. Their voices mingle. Alice stops singing.*)

Why, I guess you're finished. (*Sparky rolls his eyes.*) You're a damn pig, Sparky.

Flyin' West

PEARL CLEAGE

(Miss Leah, a nineteenth-century black pioneer in Kansas, is a leader in her community. She is talking to a group of other women.)

MISS LEAH: It's a messy business, shootin' folks. It ain't like killin' a hog, you know. Sheriff has to come. White folks have to come. All that come with shootin' somebody.

But folks die all kinds of ways. Sometimes they be goin' along just as nice as you please and they heart just give out. Just like that. Don't nobody know why. Things just happen. (*A beat*) One day a little bit before I left the plantation, Colonel Harrison bought him a new cook. Ella. She was a big strong woman. She didn't make no trouble either. Just worked hard and kept to herself. Ella knew a lot about herbs. What to put in to make it taste good. Colonel Harrison just love the way she cook. He used to let her roam all over the plantation pickin' wild herbs to put in her soups and stews. And she wouldn't tell nobody what she use. Said it was secrets from Africa. White folks didn't need to know. Colonel Harrison just laugh. He was eatin' good and didn't care 'bout where it come from no way.

But after a while, that overseer started messin' around her. Tryin' to get Colonel Harrison to let him have his way with her, but Colonel Harrison said no and told him to stay from around her. She belonged in the kitchen. But that ol' overseer still wanted her and everybody knew next time he had a chance, he was gonna get her.

So one day, Colonel Harrison went to town. Gonna be gone all day. So that overseer put some poor colored man in charge of our misery and walked on up to the house like he was the master now 'cause Colonel Harrison gone off for the day. And when he walk up on the back porch, he had one thing on his mind, but Ella had been up early, too, and the first thing he saw before he even saw her was a fresh apple pie coolin' in the window. And it smelled so good, he almost forgot what he come for. And Ella opened the screen door and smile like he the person she wanna see most in this world and she ask him if he'd like a glass of cold milk and a piece of her hot apple pie. Of course he did! What man wouldn't? And he sat down there and she cut him a big ol' piece and she told him it was hot and to be careful not to burn hisself. . . . And do you know what happened? Well, he didn't even get to finish that piece of pie Ella cut for him so pretty. Heart just stopped right in the middle of a great big bite. By the time the master got back, they had him laid out in the barn and Ella was long gone. (*A beat*) But she did do one last thing before she left. She gave me her recipe for apple pie.

Philomela's Tapestry

ALICE EVE COHEN

(Jessica talks to the audience while her cervix is being examined and filmed by Dr. Cooperman and his staff for his presentation on DES daughters.)

JESSICA: So I'm suddenly gripped with this fear that while Dr. Cooperman is filming my gigantically magnified cervix, I will become profoundly . . . small . . . microscopic. And I am somehow utterly convinced that the only way to save myself from this humbling form of annihilation is to get Dr. Cooperman to laugh. (*Singing, from Gilbert & Sullivan*) "A wandering *menstrual* I, a thing of shreds and patches" . . . Heh-heh . . . heh . . .

Speaking of menstruation, when I was eleven years old, my mother said (*Caricatured voice*), "Sweetheart, soon you'll be a young woman, and you'll—you'll start—BLEEDING every month, and you'll have to wear sanitary napkins," but she neglected to mention exactly *where* I'd be bleeding from, so I figured I'd bleed from *everywhere,* and that every month I'd have to go to school mummified from head to foot in napkins—*very clean napkins*—*boiled* napkins—so I wouldn't bleed all over my sixth-grade classroom. Thank you, I am overwhelmed; thank you for giving me this standing ovulation.

Of course, my mother had a lot of difficulty naming parts (*Gestures to her crotch*)—private parts—and thus my privates remained nameless. But to be perfectly fair, can you really expect your mother to say, "Well . . . Sweetheart, since I'm sure you want to know, this is called your labia, plus your mound of Venus, plus your clitoris, plus your urethra, plus your vagina, and it's a place of love and sex and childbirth and blood and pleasure and passion and pain and ecstasy, and there's no easy single name for the sum total of this intimate geography you can cover with one hand. Suffice it to say, Darling, that the WHOLE is greater than the sum of your parts. No pun intended."

But in retrospect, to fully prepare me for the realities of colloquial language and attitude, my mother should have said, "Darling, in time you'll hear it called 'pussy' and 'clit' and 'slit' and 'hole' and 'twat,' and you-the-person will be seen as nothing but a giant fig leaf covering the 'CUNT,' but you must remember that the Divine Place you're covering with your hand is the gate to the Sacred Temple of the Moon Goddess, and is too sacred and powerful to be named."

But that's ridiculous. A vagina's just a vagina.

Scavengers

KAREN CRONACHER

(Jeanne speaks to the audience from her living room that is littered with junk collected from antique shops, dusty books, dirty clothes, dying plants, and dirty ashtrays.)

JEANNE: I live my life like I'm a movie star, everyone's eyes on me, me, me, cameras rolling, motors whirring, shutters clicking; at every moment, visions of me being formed. (*She sits up, strikes a pose.*)

I sense the camera trailing me like a hound, I feel the hunger of the camera's eye as it devours me.

The first time I feel the camera's eye on me I'm fifteen years old living in this totalitarian regime otherwise known as Lloyd Harbor, Long Island. My spirit is festering, it's looking for a way to explode out of the cracks in the pavement of the even driveways, it's looking to bloom forth out of a pampered lawn like a gigantic weed of a resistant strain. But everything's so clean and comfortable and convenient that the spirit can't come out right. When it does come out it's taken an ugly, twisted, blackened form. And the camera finds me just as I'm submitting to this dark thing.

Suddenly I can't keep my eyes away from men's crotches. A little voice inside me is whispering, I dare you to look there, just for second, he won't notice, go on, look there, and I have to look. No man is spared. I'm called into the principal's office for tormenting the lunch ladies—I don't remember how I tortured them—and as the principal is asking how a nice young honor student like me has developed the nasty habit of torturing lunch ladies, I'm staring at his crotch waiting to see if he'll notice.

Then I'm drinking like a fiend, all the time, especially during school. In A.P. English we're studying Poe and while someone's reading a poem aloud I stand up, drunk as a lark, my arms flailing, and I'm pointing at some crows outside screaming, "THEY'RE HERE! THE RAVENS HAVE DESCENDED! THEY'RE CRASHING THROUGH THE WINDOW PANE!" At about this time I'm refusing to ride the school bus on moral grounds.

At about this time I go to the Homecoming Dance—stag, of course—oh, I drank till I thought I was dead, dead, dead—and I start dancing all by myself, I'm twirling around faster and faster until everyone else stops dancing to stare at me because my body is twisting and contorting like I'm a dying animal and ever so accidently I step on the Homecoming Queen's toe with my pointy, pointy heel until I've embedded the spike in her nail—crunch! And she can't dance and she has to hobble through her parade and they take me home and strip me and put me to bed and make my little sister stay by me all night long so I won't choke on my own vomit—and around about this time I receive a little pink slip in homeroom which says, "The school psychiatrist would like an appointment with YOU" and he's telling me I have this death drive as I stare at his crotch and I'm telling him I live my life out of passion, like the stars, I'm telling him I lead two lives, one for me and one for the camera's eye, I'm telling him in fourth grade the boys stole my mittens and they *still* haven't given them back, I'm telling him there's a malnourished spirit seeping out of me, coming out ankles first, I'm telling him there's a scavenger of love drinking my sweet sticky blood out of cracked cups and he just stares at me hard and says, "Suzy's toenail turned black and fell off." "I bet her skin is the color of seashells underneath" I say and he asks me why I'm so unhappy and can't we meet twice a week from now on and I'm enchanted, I'm enchanted by the thought of the tender pink flesh of Suzy's toe newly exposed.

So I was in this store in the city, buying the . . . you know, and all of a sudden I'm really aware of the surveillance, and it starts to . . . well, it starts to turn me on. I'm watching the camera gently pan the store, and I want it to focus in on me for a close-up, but it keeps panning. So I start to walk around the store, always within its range. I'm walking back and forth in a semi-circle, and it's following me. It's a real high, you know? And then I get this urge to really hold its interest, give it something to pan about. So I steal this thing. . . . There's no sense in *buying* a thing like that, you know, it's none of the salesladies' business anyway, I mean, what happens in the bedroom is a very private kind of thing.

Then I go to the Metropolitan Museum of Art, and some guard is trying to force me to give him a donation, so I'm fumbling around for change in my big open bag and I drop the bag and the thing falls out like a great black spider on the white marble floor and there's dead silence in the lobby of the Met as everyone turns away from the pictures to look at my thing spread out on the floor. And everyone in the Met starts laughing. They all start laughing because that's the kind of thing they really want to see. They're laughing because they don't really care about some dead pictures once owned by some dead rich people hanging on a wall. And then everyone joins hands and starts dancing in a circle, the guards and the intellectuals and the artists and the bums on the street, men, women, and children—we're all dancing in a circle of love around my thing, and we're skipping past the Egyptian mummies, and we're skipping past the primitive weapons, and we're skipping into the big cafe with the dolphin pool, and we all form a circle in the pool and we're splashing around and laughing and throwing the pennies in the air, the day there was art in the Met!

Rose

EDWIDGE DANTICAT

(The speaker, a Haitian woman, has lived in Scarsdale, New York, for six months.)

She was very pretty. Bright shiny hair and dark brown skin like mahogany cocoa. Her lips were thick and purple, like those African dolls you see in white store windows, but could never afford to buy.

I thought she was a gift from Heaven when I saw her on the sidewalk, wrapped in a small pink blanket, a few inches from the curb. Like baby Moses in the Bible stories they read to us at the Methodist English class. Or baby Jesus who was born in a barn and died on a cross with nobody's lips to kiss when he went. She was like that. Her still round face. Her eyes closed as though she was dreaming of another place.

Her hands were bony and there were veins so close to the surface that you could rupture them if you touched her too hard.

She probably belonged to someone, but the street had no one in it.

I was afraid to touch her. Lest I might disturb the early morning rays, sun rays, streaming across her forehead. Maybe she was some kind of *wanga*, an illusion fixed to trap me. My enemies were many and crafty. The girls who slept with my husband while I was grieving my miscarriages. They might have sent that vision of loveliness to pull me back to a place that I totally killed within myself when I got on that boat in Port-au-Prince, six months ago.

She was wearing an embroidered little green dress with the letters R-O-S-E on the butterfly collar.

She looked the way I'd imagined all my little girls would look. The ones my body could never hold. The ones that somehow got suffocated inside me and made my husband wonder if I was killing them on purpose.

I called out all the names I had wanted to give them. Helene, Nicolette, Malene, Laflorette, Nadine, Jacqueline, Karine.

I could give her all the clothes I'd sewn for them. All these little dresses that went unused. I could rock her in silence in the middle of the night, rest her on my belly, wishing she were inside.

I saw on the TV once that a lot of poor black American girls throw out their babies. On door steps, in garbage bags, gas stations, sidewalks. In the two months I'd been in Scarsdale, I had never seen such a child, until now.

But, Rose. My, she was so clean. Like a tiny angel, sleeping after the wind had blown a lullaby into her little ears.

I picked her up and pressed her cheek against mine. I felt her coldness.

"Little Rose," I whispered as though her name were a secret.

She was like the edible little puppets we played with as children—mangoes we drew faces on and then called by our nicknames.

She didn't stir or cry, and somehow I knew she never would. She was like something that was thrown aside after she became useless to someone.

When I pressed her face against my heart, she smelled like the scented powders in Madame's cabinet.

Loud in My Head

EVE ENSLER

(Artemis cleans public toilets.)

ARTEMIS: I am cleaning a toilet. What you see is correct. I am inside it, with my gloved hand cleaning. I clean the toilet for money. You might call me a toilet bowl cleaner. You might call me a toilet bowl worker. You might call me a woman, dark woman with Ajax in her hand. You are probably surprised at my ability to articulate. You are even disturbed by my precise diction. You expected the toilet bowl cleaner to sound like the toilet, all gurgling and swallowing. You expected the toilet bowl cleaner to have already dissolved into the endless wiping and splashing, to have become as dumb and expressionless as the porcelain. You did not expect a person cleaning a toilet bowl to have read Charles Dickens or Franz Kafka or Virginia Woolf. You did not expect the dark woman to read in the bathroom, to read compulsively while she was cleaning the toilet bowl. (*Artemis resumes cleaning the toilet.*)

This is a hole where feces goes, where piss goes and vomit and blood. This is a hole where waste disappears and bad moments and lies. This is a hole that swallows what no one sees, what no one talks about. This is a shit hole, a crap hole, a turd hole, a big brown hole, a frog dropping hole, a doody hole, a caa caa hole, a stink hole, a BM hole. You could get lost here. You could get bit. Birds, big black birds live here, pecking your ass, pecking holes, blood holes into your soft exposed ass.

I am cleaning. I am cleaning the entrance to the hole. Noble entrance cleaner. Cleaning the way. Creating a path, nice white porcelain path. Nice Ajax absorbing the brown, absorbing the stain, the memory. Absorbing the evidence. Absorbing the hurt of it, the residue of it, the practical reality of it, the poison, the disturbance of it, the truth of it. The document shredded, the semen dried, the fingerprints wiped. Clean toilet. Clean files. Clean money. Cleaning. You pay me to clean. I am a cleaner. You might say I create the future. You might say I censor the past. You might call me assassin. Dirt assassin. Stink assassin. Paid assassin. Killing your stains.

The uptight ones can't do it with me in the room. They sit in there for a long time hoping I'll go away. Then when they try I can hear them holding it in. They're scared I'll report them to the Fart Police. (*Becomes Police*) Come out of there with your hands up—you're under arrest. Come out or we'll break the door down. (*Little voice*) No officer, wait, wait. (*Police*) Reports have it that four big stinky ones came out of that stall. POOP POLICE.

Then there's the other ones, the real pretty ones. The self involved comb their hair over the sinks, glued to the mirror ones. They're not worried about the fart police or the litter police or the human police. They're pretty. They fart and stink and drop their Moddess pads and ask you for anything. Safety pins, pine deodorant, Tampax, vitamins, change. Do I look like a drugstore? Just call me Bessie Rexall, Diana Reade.

Then there's what I call the guilty girls. Those girls are guilty about just about everything. They're sorry you're a cleaning lady, sorry they discovered pee on their toilet seat, sorry they were the ones that had to tell you, sorry there's any pee in the world at all, sorry they're not cleaning pee, but they're lawyers, sorry. They ask questions about your personal life and this relieves their guilt because they feel like they're having a relationship with you, except they're too guilty about how much money they make so they don't tell you anything about themselves. You're like their monkey puppet. They get deep into your business. How much do you make? Did your husband leave you? They talk about organizing. They're great champions of your cause and you haven't even asked them. And when you tell them you don't have time to organize, you work, they act like you're one big failure of a human being, no Norma Rae here. Then they get pissy and they quit you and all their guilt gets momentarily gone and they feel better. I've got to calm down. I'll talk about my products. I love my products. I have product admiration. I could do a commercial. It would be sincere. People would buy my products. People would admire me for my love of my products. I believe, for example, in Fantastik. It is close to an ideology, my belief. I believe in Fantastik because it fulfills what it promises. "Gets dirt off anything in one easy motion." I love that "one easy motion." When I spray Fantastik on anything, anything gets better. Anything ventures into the mysterious, the challenging, the petty, the impossible, frustrating and sometimes grandiose. Anything could be your arm. Anything could be a dead cat, a fried tomato, broken glass, a pink slipper, a porcelain bowl. See your face shine, Fantastik glow. Anything could be your nightmares, your neighbor, your linoleum floor. I believe in products because they work, because they do what they say. Because their bottle life is limited, because the results are clear. Products are not people. Products are truthful. You can hold them in your hand.

I'm about to have a mood change. I need it. I need to change this low-down dragging ass can't do it no more mood. It stinks here in the smelly old turd hole. Ammonia passing through brain cells, broken cement floors that never get cleaned. I'm ABOUT TO CHANGE IT, ALWAYS WANTED TO CHANGE IT. I'm about to get happy, get happy. Maybe there's something coming. Maybe this is just the dream part and the wake-up's coming. I'm about to get a poke, a punch, a push, a yes, a yes. I'm about to believe again. I'm about to be a believer. You can count on it. We can all count on it. Hallelujah! *Snickers. (Artemis takes out a big Snickers bar from her pocket.)*

It's a Snickers bar. It's love, a love bar, a Snickers pocket size bar, a Snickers friend. A loving friend. It's candy. It's love. It's custom. It's love. It's friendly, Snickers. It's waiting for me, warm in my pocket. It's waiting like the beginning, always waiting. Oh yes, warm milky chocolate bar, warm milky soft baby bar, warm chocolate galaxy, melting like the sun with goodness. LOVE. How I imagined it, tasted it. Mama. I'm about to. . . . Six Snickers in my pocket. Six mood changes per day. Six possibilities. Six beginnings. Six friends. Six prayers. Six presents. In my pocket. Used to eat all of them at once. All six, all at once. All warm love and soft love and nutty love going in. All little brown wrappers opening. One huge amount of hope. One gigantic leap forward. I'm an astronaut, a cowgirl, an opera star. All six pulsing into the bloodstream—pushing and pumping and winning. But then I'd black out. I'm disciplined now. I carefully distribute my happiness throughout the day. It is adult happiness. Well thought out practical happiness. It is not as much happiness at once. But it is something to look forward to—something that's coming.

Consequences

KATHLEEN GERMANN

I know what I should be thinking right now, but what I'm really thinking is: Okay, so what, when it's over will he stay the night or will he think up some excuse as to why he has to leave? And if he does leave will it be right after, or will he wait until I fall asleep and then just sneak out?

But maybe he won't leave. Maybe he will stay the night. Then I'll have to see him in the morning. What if he's really ugly in the morning? Do I have to kiss him right away or can I brush my teeth first? But what about him? I know he doesn't have a toothbrush here and he's not going to share mine.

And then what about breakfast? What if he expects me to make him breakfast? Or worse, what if he wants to make breakfast? Should I let him? I mean I don't want him to think I can't cook. "She's a great lay. Too bad she can't scramble an egg."

So I evaluate these things in my mind and make little compromises. If the sex is great, I'll cook. Omelettes, juice, toast, coffee, the whole nine yards. If he's just so-so, I'll let him cook, see how he fares on Teflon. If he's not so good, there's a Dunkin' Donuts around the corner.

But let's assume for a moment that everything's great. The sex is fantastic, the best I've ever had. Breakfast is fantastic, the best I've ever had. He kisses me sweetly good-bye (he carries breath mints) leaving me to bask in the glow of the aftermath.

Is he gonna call me? And if he does, when? I mean, I don't want it to be too soon, I don't want him to be eager. But don't wait three days either. We just made love and now he waits half a week to call me! Who the fuck does he think he is? Who the fuck does he think I am—a disposable human being? Just do her and dump her? And what is he gonna say, "Thanks, it's been great, let's do it again some time."—Go fuck yourself next time—

You see, that's the difference between men and women. Men are only concerned with immediate gratification. Women think about the long-range consequences.

Birthday

JOLENE GOLDENTHAL

(On her 47th birthday, Kitty talks to her mother. During the speech, she has several strong drinks, while running back and forth from the phone to the mirror, to the window, to the closet, to the bar.)

KITTY: It's my birthday. Not your birthday. . . . my birthday. Oh God! Can't you remember anything? *(Pleading)* Say Happy Birthday. Happy Birthday, Kitty. . . . Say it, Mamma . . . Please! *(After a pause, patiently)* I know you're miserable. I didn't want to put you there. You've got to believe me. It was Lenny. Lenny loves you, Mamma. He was worried about you all the time. He went to work and couldn't think. . . . He couldn't do his work . . . worrying about you. . . . maybe turning on the stove . . . and forgetting all about it. . . . Or wandering around in the street . . . without a coat . . . maybe getting hit by a car. . . . Lenny worried a lot about you. . . . He . . . he really loves you, Mamma. In his way. . . . *(Pause)* Well yes, . . . it's true. You could have stayed here with us. . . . *(Low)* Lenny didn't want you, Mamma. He . . . he thought it would be too much work for me . . . I guess. . . . *(Brief pause)* Oh the Hell with it. . . . He didn't want you! HE DIDN'T WANT YOU IN HIS HOUSE! Old . . . and sick . . . and smelly. . . . Lenny hates old people. He hates the idea of being old. He hates knowing that he's growing old. . . . *(An attempt at cheerfulness)* Listen, I'm going to have a little drink. Just a tiny little drink . . . to celebrate my birthday. . . . I'm going to pretend you're here with me. . . . And we're going to drink to my birthday. *(Relaxed, after a stiff drink from an open bottle of whisky)* I wish you could remember my birthday. . . . It's like

34

I was never born when my own mother can't remember my birthday. . . . (*Drinks*) It's a big one, too. (*Small pause*) I'm gonna think about . . . I'm gonna concentrate on my birthday. . . . *(Smiling)* I'm gonna make my birthday . . . a party. Nobody else gonna make it. . . . I'm gonna make it. (*Shouting happily into the phone*) You wanna come to my party? (*Then ignoring the phone*) I'm gonna have . . . cake . . . and . . . surprises . . . and lots a stuff. . . . Bought myself a birthday present. . . . Nobody else . . . gonna give me a present. . . . Gonna have a nice surprise present. . . . Gonna look great for my birthday. . . . Mamma . . . I'm gonna look nice for my birthday! (*Small pause*) I thought you'd like that. I'll look nice . . . and pretty. . . . (Small pause) Everybody always said I was pretty. . . . (*Anxious*) I was a pretty girl, wasn't I? (*Low, to herself*) Everybody said . . . I was a pretty girl. . . . I'm going to wear my new red tunic. . . . And my black silk pants . . . and my red sandals . . . and my dangly earrings . . . that Lenny gave me . . . last year. . . . *(Sobbing)* I'm going to look gorgeous! *(Calling)* I'm going to have a party. . . . Will you come to my party. . . . (*Talking to nobody*) It's going to be a fantastic party! I'm going to wear my red satin tunic and my shiny black pants . . . and my red sandals. . . . (*Calling wildly, distractedly*) We'll have caviar! And champagne! And music! And flowers! And people. . . . Lots and lots of people! Everybody. ALL MY FRIENDS! *(Build)* I'll laugh . . . with my friends . . . and they'll drink a toast . . . to my birthday. . . . And they'll wish me many . . . many more. . . . Many more. . . . (*Low*) It's my birthday, Mamma. Can you wish me a Happy Birthday? Please . . . Mamma . . . please. . . .

LIVERPOOL JOHN MOORES UNIVERSITY
Aldham Robarts L.R.C.
TEL. 051 231 3701/3634

Margaret's Workout

JANE HILL

(In her late forties, Margaret wears a drab uniform-like dress and flat shoes. She stands behind a chair. Nearby, a poster on a large easel reads: MID-LIFE: ISSUES & ANSWERS.)

MARGARET: Hello. My name is Margaret Thatcher. No. Not that one. I mean, I would love to be her. She really has it together, you know what I mean? So certain. Well, to tell the truth, I hate her politics. But I admire her certainty. They may push her out, but they can't get rid of her. She's a fine example of a mature, competent woman. Everything about her is definite. You can tell by her hair. It looks positively shellacked. Not that I'm against flexibility. Especially for hair. Thank you. That WAS a little joke.

(*Apologetic*) I know it's hard to tell now when I'm joking. It's like this big grey pile of sludge has settled down over everything—even my sense of humor—which, believe it or not, is still functioning somewhere under the sludge. I tried to explain that to Sidney—my therapist. How this thing I did—this "horrible thing"—really just started as a kind of joke. And I admit it got away from me. (*Wistfully*) But even now when I think about it, parts of it still seem funny to me. That's probably not a good sign. Anyway, I'm getting off track here. And I'm trying to work on that. Stay on track. Stay in control, you know? It was Sidney's idea that I come here to talk to you about my "incident." Well, really about the events that led up to it. Because it's relevant to your conference topic. (*Indicates sign*) "MID-LIFE: ISSUES AND ANSWERS." Well, let's get one thing straight right away. I don't have any of the answers. Issues, that's another matter.

(*Takes a deep breath and lets it out*) So! Where to begin? I guess I'll just start with some facts. Though to tell you the truth, facts don't really explain much. Well, I'm gonna stay on track here, so . . . facts. (*Indicates her garb*) Seeing me now you might not be able to tell—and I guess you're just gonna have to take my word for it—I had a pretty successful life. A career—executive director of a small social service agency. They don't want to be dragged through the mud any more, so I won't mention which one. Three kids. Nice. No big problems. Nice husband—Jack, a real go-getter. Built his insurance agency into a multi-million dollar operation. I had a lovely home in the suburbs. The whole bit. And I knew—I mean I read *Cosmo*—that the middle years could be difficult for some people. So I planned ahead. Thought about the issues. "Empty Nest Syndrome." "Plastic Surgery." "Middle-age Spread." I even planned my first mid-life pajama crisis. Made a pajama party out of it with two of my girlfriends. Well, it was kind of a joke in a way. But in a way it wasn't.

My first kid had just left home. Which was great, because she was off doing what she wanted to do, and I've always encouraged my children to be independent. But I didn't expect to miss her so much. I didn't realize that in those days I actually spent more time with her than with Jack. His business demanded a lot of his attention. It wasn't a problem. I understood. We had good communication. But Nancy was the one I was close to. The one I talked to about my ideas and concerns and interests.

So I had this mid-life crisis pajama party. And I made a plan. A plan to do more things for myself. Lose weight. Join a gym. Get my hair done more often. Eat tofu. Lose weight. Oh, I said that, didn't I? Because to tell you the truth, our sex life had gotten a little bogged down. Jack was tired a lot. And I had let myself get a little—well, you know. But despite all the good things I was doing for myself, this kind of vaguely anxious gray feeling settled over me. So I had my hormones checked. And they were fine, according to my doctor. Up till then I used to joke about menopause. You know, like "Where do I sign up?" And how it would be great to spend that money on manicures instead of tampons. I mean, do you realize how much we women spend on sanitary products over the course of a lifetime? Mindboggling.

My doctor gave me a pamphlet. "Menopause and You." And it explained how menopause is not a disease, it's just a normal, natural part of life. And what the symptoms are for this thing that isn't a disease. I didn't think I had any of them. Well, one had me a little stumped. "Vaginal dryness." Because at that point, Jack and I hadn't made love in two years. So how could I tell?

I mean we did talk about it. Our lack of amorous activity. And Jack was really honest about it. He explained that I just didn't fit his picture of a desirable woman. Oh, he loved me. Respected me. Wanted to care for me. I am really an incredibly wonderful human being, according to Jack. He blamed the problem on his being a typical American male caught up in all that "image-of-woman" stuff. You know, *Playboy* centerfolds, nineteen-year-old blondes. . . . You get the picture. And he swore he wasn't playing around or anything. He just couldn't get excited about *me*. You could tell he felt really bad about it. He admitted it really was sexual immaturity on his part. Because, after all, everyone grows older. And gravity is the common enemy, if you know what I mean. And he didn't want to go to a counselor or anything, because he really didn't think it was worth it. Anyway, that was how he felt. And we both agreed, it really was *his* problem. (*Pause*) So why did *I* feel so shitty? And old. And tired. And undesirable.

But I knew I should not let this get me down. So I went to my aerobics class as usual. And the music was really loud. And I was leaping and pumping and sweating with all the rest of the gals. When suddenly I caught my own eye in the mirror. And I had this . . . just "dead" look, you know? Nobody home. In the glass I could see about thirty other women reflected. The pretty young girls looked so happy.

Like it was really fun. And the older women were flushed. Some of them looked kind of panicked. A couple of them couldn't keep up. Then I got this funny idea.

I stopped jumping up and down and walked over to my gym bag and pulled out my really great butane curling iron. No cord, you know? It's completely portable. And I walked towards the front of the gym, across the purple carpet. The neon lights were flashing on the wall in time to the music. I went past the instructor—who looked sort of surprised. And I took my curling iron and began smashing the wall mirrors. Smashing and crashing all those images. The pretty young ones—who had no idea what was waiting for them. And the old lumpy ones, who knew, maybe, but didn't dare talk about it. And who had to be let out, you see. Out of the mirrors. It wasn't fair. Someone had to set them free. And I knew I could do it.

But they didn't understand, I guess. And people started screaming and running. And some of them fell down. In the mirror that still stuck to the wall I could see the real people coming apart, too. Tumbling and screaming and not knowing they could be quiet now. And very calm. Like me.

Then a piece of glass came away from the wall and cut me. Right through my shiny new Danskin leotard. Royal blue. And it looked kind of nice, the red and the blue. So I dropped the curling iron—which was pretty bent by now— and I took a big shard of the glass and began slashing my leotard all over. It was pretty funny in a way. So I started to laugh. And when I ran out of leotard, I started on my hair.

(*Pause*) When I came to, I was in Mercy Hospital and people were asking me all these weird questions. Like, "Why had I done it?" And it was so simple really. So I didn't answer them. But it was nothing personal against Jane Fonda, like one of the papers said.

That was three months ago. They called it a nervous breakdown. Now I'm at a different hospital where I'm supposed to spend a lot of time talking to Sidney. You remember, my therapist? But to tell you the truth, I don't tell him much. As a matter of fact, I've discovered quite a lot about Sidney.

He was featured in an article in the local paper, "Movers and Shakers in Your Neighborhood." He's forty-eight. He has silver hair and a neat mustache. He does those Nautilus exercises. He drives a Porsche. His new wife is twenty-seven. I just don't think he'd get it.

Still Blooming

JANE HILL

(Shirley Wrinkle is very old and feeble, but still has a formidable presence. She wears flat-heeled tap shoes and supports herself with a four-legged aluminum walker. On each leg of the walker is a tiny white sock and a baby-sized patent leather shoe.)

SHIRLEY: Good afternoon. I'm Shirley Wrinkle. The world's oldest living tap dancer. I'm one hundred and three. (*Pause*) All right. One hundred and ten. The world forgives a woman for lying about her age. Awright, awright. I'm only ninety-two. But nobody's interested in an old woman unless she's over a hundred. Not even Willard Scott. I want to thank Mrs. Moore, the chairman of your entertainment committee, for inviting me here today to share some reflections about my long and fascinating life. And I'm going to let you in on a few important secrets I've discovered.

For example, some of you have already noticed I use a walker. There are two ways to look at a walker. If there are any "New Age" types here, it's kind of like the "half-empty/half-full" glass analogy. Well, never mind. The walker. Two ways to look at it. You can see it as a sign of your physical deterioration. Or you can see it for what it really is. An opportunity for four more tap shoes.

Please don't think I'm being brave. Crap, no! I'm being realistic. (*Looks around cautiously and waves sweetly to someone in the audience*) Sorry, Estelle. I forgot and used the "C" word. Estelle brought me here in the hospital van. She's on the staff. For "By-the-Sea Convalescent Care Home." Practically overlooks the Pacific, if you can see that far. It's a

41

lovely place. Charming. No, really. Of course, the residents call it the "Bide-a-Wee." Why? Because no one expects to stay long. And yet no one actually believes they'll die, do they? Oops, now I did it. I used the "D" word.

But I didn't mean to digress. You aren't here to listen to my views of death. I have two areas of expertise. Two reasons why the "Bide-a-Wee" management takes me on these little jaunts to share my gifts with the general public. I am, as I stated, the world's oldest living tap dancer. But I also know a lot about romance. That's a hot topic these days. What exactly is romance, you wonder? It's the Yuppie version of love. The cleaned-up version of sex. And I've spent many years reflecting on it.

I've been in love. The first time I was seventeen. The last time—let me amend that—the most *recent* time, I was eighty-three. He was a beast. All he thought about was sex, sex, sex. You look confused, madam. Do I mean seventeen or eighty-three? Both! Yes, it's a popular misconception that the elderly are not interested in sex any more. Don't you believe it. It causes a lot of problems at the "Bide-a-Wee." Romance blooms, but it's nipped in the bud by Sominex.

I've been married six times. Well, you don't get to be an expert without a lot of research, I always say. I married for love each time. My first husband, Alfredo, was a performer with an Italian circus. There's something about a man in spangled tights that's just irresistible. I grew up in a small town in western Pennsylvania. One of those dreary coal mining towns, you know? But I always knew I was destined for a career in show business. The week the circus stayed in our town I attended every performance. By the end of the week, I knew every routine by heart. Alfredo's act was the most exciting. He was shot out of a real cannon. No mirror tricks, you know! Boom! And off he went. It was thrilling.

I always ran out to see where he landed. Always the same spot. This pile of foam padding. He never missed. Well, once. But that's another part of my story. You see, when the circus left town, I went with them. By then I was completely smitten. And within two months, Alfredo and I were married. I soon became part of the show, helping with the act. My job—in a glamorous costume, of course—was to load the cannon with the exact amount of powder required. And then, on an exciting musical crescendo, to touch a torch to the charge. I learned just how to build the suspense. For a year, we were happy as two little pigeons. And then I discovered Alfredo was unfaithful. In fact, he had several other wives in the small towns on our tour circuit.

That's when the accident happened. One night something went wrong with the powder charge. There was a huge explosion and Alfredo sailed into the night sky. I remember there was a full moon . . . his spangled tights glittering and glistening, his beautiful body silhouetted against the moon. He never did come down. Or at least we never discovered where. It was a spectacular finish to the act, of course.

Personally, I think Alfredo was lucky. He didn't outlast our love. Each time I've been in love, I've had a similar reaction. A sort of death wish. Now that's not cynical. It's realistic. Because we live in the nineties, for God's sake. We've screwed up just about everything. The air. The water. The rain forest. So you tell me. . . . You're in love, the most sublime of states. What do you wish for? The end of the world, if you're smart. Who in their right mind would want to survive love?

And romance? Ah, romance! Unlike love, romance lasts. Romance is the residue of love. (*Spotting a particular audience member*) Ah, I saw that smile. You know what I'm talking about. Well, I won't betray you. We romantics have to stick together. When people find out about us, they won't leave us alone. They feel compelled to try and "burst the bubble." Keep trying to convince you that the actual experience was better than the memory. What nonsense! Our only defense is to pretend we're senile. Just don't listen. Take up crafts. Knitting is good. Look carefully at the next knitter you see. They usually have a little smile on their face. Knit one, purl two. (*She demonstrates the tiny smile of the "secret romantic."*) Sure sign of a romantic.

And contrary to popular opinion, most of us elderly romantics are not clinging desperately to life. Or this shabby substitute for it that's known as "old age." I once had a dear friend at the "Bide-a-Wee," Eunice Wilson. She was in terrible shape. Lots of pain. One day she said to me, "Shirley, I just don't get it. I've cleaned up all the odds and ends of my life. I seem to be just hanging around here, taking up space. Why can't I die?"

Well, as a matter of fact, this particular woman was quite a resource for everyone else at the "Bide-a-Wee." She was sharp as a tack. Anyhow, in her day, Eunice had been a great gardener. And she liked to be turned in her bed so she could look out at this little plot of flowers next to the hospital. So, a few days later, I shuffled in to see her. She was in her usual position, gazing out the window. She said, "Shirley, I've figured out why I can't die yet. I'm still blooming."

(*Notices Estelle again*) Well, I see that Estelle is giving me the high sign, so it's time for my number. Hit it, Estelle. (*Piano intro begins to the tune of "Tea for Two." Follow spot comes on, if available.*)

Picture me, the "Bide-a-Wee"
Just tea for one and one for tea
Just me myself, just me with me alone.
Nobody near me to see me or hear me,
No friends or relations on weekend vacations,
I won't have it known, dear,
That I can't afford a phone, dear.
Day will break and I'll awake,
My joints may ache
But still I'll make
An effort to have fun, to still be me!
I've outlived my family,
But I've no time for misery,
Can't you see what's bloomin' here is me?!

(*Dance break. Shirley executes a halting tap dance routine with her own tap shoes and those of the walker.*)
I've outlived my family,
But I've no time for misery,
Can't you see what's bloomin' here—it's me!
(*Takes her bows, then begins waving to Estelle*) That's right, Estelle, you get the van warmed up while I say goodnight to the nice people. Sssshhh! Sssshhh! I got to talk fast here. I don't know crap about tap dancing. You got all nostalgic, because you thought my aged infirmities had diminished my abilities. Baloney! I only started studying this stuff six months ago. When I got the walker! It was an inspired idea—my ticket out of the "Bide-a-Wee" a couple of times a month. I took the med-car. Everyone thought I was going to the doctor, but I scooted around the corner to my tap teacher. Well, I'm not ashamed to be a subversive.

As a tap dancer I confess I'm a fake. A fraud. A beginner. But I've always wanted to do it. You know what it is for me? And this is the *real* secret I came here to share with you. It's a fierce embrace of physicality. So what if it's only from the ankles down! Don't let anybody talk you into giving that up. Get the message. Keep blooming!
(*Song reprise without piano accompaniment or follow spot*)
I've outlived my family,
But I've no time for misery.
Can't you see what's bloomin' here—that's me!

Teeth

TINA HOWE

(Amy is having a filling replaced at her dentist's office. During this monologue, the dentist is on the floor, trying with increasing desperation to open a bottle of cement.)

AMY: I keep having this recurring nightmare. I just wonder if you've heard it before. I have it at least three times a week now. I wake up exhausted with my whole jaw throbbing. Waa . . . waa . . . waa! You know, the old . . . TEETH-GRANULATING-ON-YOU-DREAM! (*She stifles a sob.*) You're at a party, flashing a perfect smile when suddenly you hear this splintering sound like someone smashing teacups in the next room . . . ping . . . tock . . . crackkkkkkkkkk . . . tinkle, tinkle. . . . "Well, someone's having a good time!" you say to yourself expecting to see some maniac swinging a sledgehammer. So you casually look around, and of course there *is* no maniac! . . . Then you feel these prickly shards clinging to your lips. . . . You try and brush them away, but suddenly your mouth is filled with them. You can't spit them out fast enough! (*She tries, spitting and wiping.*) People are starting to stare. . . . You try to save face. (*To the imagined party-goers*) "Well, what do you know . . . I seem to have taken a bite out of my coffee cup! Silly me!" (*She laughs, frantically wiping.*) Then I catch a glimpse of myself in the mirror. . . . You got it! My teeth are spilling out of my mouth in little pieces. I frantically try and moosh them back in, but there's nothing to hold onto. Then they start granulating on me . . . fsssssssssssssss . . . It's like trying to build a sand castle inside an hour glass! My mouth is a blaze of gums. We are talking pink for *miles* . . . ! Magellan staring out over the Pacific Ocean during a sunset in 1520—(*As Magellan*) "Pink . . . pink . . . pink . . . pink!" What does it *mean*, is what I'd like to know! I mean, teeth are supposed to last forever, right? They hold up through floods, fires, earthquakes and wars . . . the one part of us that endures. So if they granulate on you, where does that leave you? *Nowhere!* You could have been rain or wind for all anybody knows. That's pretty scary. . . . (*Starting to get weepy*) One minute you're laughing at a party and the next you've evaporated into thin air. . . . (*Putting on a voice*) "Remember Amy? Gee, I wonder whatever happened to her?" (*In another voice*) "Gosh, it's suddenly gotten awfully chilly in here. Where's that *wind* coming from?" (*Teary again*) I mean, we're not around for that long as it is, so then to suddenly. . . . I'm sorry, I'm sorry. It's just that I have this um . . . long-standing . . . Oh God, here we go . . . (*Starting to break down*) Control yourself! Control . . . control! See, I have this long-standing um . . . fear of death? It's something you're born with. I used to sob in my father's arms when I was only . . . Oh boy! See, once you start thinking about it, I mean. . . . *really* thinking about it . . . You know, time going on forever and ever and ever and ever and you're not there . . . it can get pretty scary! . . . We're not talking missing out on a few measly centuries here, but boom! And back to dinosaurs again? . . . (*More and more weepy*) Eternity . . . camel trains, cities, holy wars, boom! Dinosaurs, camel trains, cities, holy wars, boom! . . . . Dinosaurs, camel trains, cities, holy wars. . . . Stop it Amy . . . just . . . *stop it!*

Little Girl Dreams

SAMANTHA GRACE KELLY

(A little girl enters carrying a baseball mitt and ball.)

LITTLE GIRL: So, I wouldn't want to play with you anyway Tommy! You suck! You suck the big one!!

I'm leaving here and I'm never coming back. I'm going to live with Dad, and you can never come visit us. I'm going to fly away.

Tommy says I can't fly a plane, but I can too. I've flown one before. It wasn't very hard. Just pretty much like driving a car, only in the air. He says girls don't fly planes, but I told him Amelia Earhart flew planes and she was a girl. He said, "Yeah, and look what happened to her. She crashed and got eaten by Japanese cannibals." But I told him she did not. She did not crash. She's living on this island off the coast of Africa now, where they made her queen. She's not dead. She escaped. They tried to get her—the Japanese men, but she escaped. I'm going to fly away like Amelia Earhart. I'll take all my things and never come back. I'll take Maxwell.

(She picks up Maxwell House coffee can.) You still in there, Maxwell? I caught a lizard. His name is Maxwell. Tommy says he's dead. He says I killed him, but I did not. I gave him a house. See, it even says "Maxwell's House" on it. He's just sleeping.

Tommy says I can't play baseball because I'm a girl. "Did you ever hear of a professional baseball player being a girl?" he says. That doesn't mean I can't play. I'm a much better hitter than he is. He says boys are better at sports, but how come I'm the fastest runner in my class then? And how come I always win at dodgeball? Girls are not weaker.

48

Once I punched Peter Dornbrush in the face and gave him a black eye. He deserved it. He was being mean to my friend Maggie, because she's fat. But I'd rather be fat than have three tits like Kenny Lipman. He does—he showed me in the closet at school. I showed him mine too. His were much bigger.

Alan asked me to marry him today during recess. But I told him I was busy today, maybe tomorrow.

We're building a bridge in the woods, over the stream, Alan and me. We made a trail between his house and mine. Now we're building a bridge. I've built most of it though.

(*Pulls bedspread over her head as if it's a wedding veil, humming the wedding march*) Dum dum de dum. Dum dum de dum . . .

My father can't walk me down the aisle if I get married. 'Cause he's dead. He lives in heaven now. They made a prayer about him at our church. "Our Father, who art in heaven. Hollow be thy name. Thy kingdom come. Thy will be done. On earth as it is in heaven. Give us this day our daily bread. And forgive us our trespasses, as we forgive those who trespass against us. And let us not into temptation, but deliver us from evil."

Maybe he could come back. Just for the wedding, then we'd send him back. Maybe God would let him.

I know where God lives. He's in my closet. I asked my mother where God lives, and she told me that God is everywhere. I said, "Even in the walls?" and she said yes. She said yes. There's this hole in the wall in my closet, and he's in there. I can't really see anything, just black. But I know he's in there. I can talk to him. He hears me. He can't really talk back too much because he's very busy. But he knows me. He knows everything.

There was a fire in the house down the road. Their whole house burned down. They lost all their worldly possessions— that means everything they own. If there was a fire in our house, Alan would save us. 'Cause he's going to be a fireman.

He won't get burned ever. Because he'll have one of those big hoses. So he can just put the fire right out. He'll ride in a big red fire engine with a really loud siren. Just like the sirens when they took my Dad away.

There were lots of policemen there. They said on the news that he was a victim of the drug war. But that's not true. He didn't do drugs. And it was just two guys fighting, not a war. And one of them had a gun. He meant to shoot the other guy, but he shot my Dad in the stomach. He wasn't in a war. He was just coming home from work. He was in advertising. He made really famous cigarette ads—even though he said smoking was bad and we should never do it.

Maggie's father works in television. She says he sells time. I told her I've never seen any ads for time on TV though. That's pretty weird anyway. I wonder what kind of people need to buy time. I always have plenty of time. I guess maybe people that are dying so they could buy enough time to find a cure for their disease.

When I grow up I'm going to be a doctor and find cures for diseases. Like Madame Curie, I think she did that.

I wish I could be an explorer, like Christopher Columbus. But now there's no more countries left to discover.

I could be an astronaut. Then I could fly into outer space and meet Martians on Mars. But they'll be good Martians, not mean ones. Ladies and Gentlemen, Betsy Malone has just landed on Mars. This is one small step for man, one giant step for . . . Betsy Malone!

I'm going to be rich and famous then. Then they'll make me into a movie star. Then I'll become really beautiful. "Here she comes, Miss America." (She parades around the room until her performance is cut short by bumping into the bed.)

Alan and I are going to have a really big house when we get married. Much bigger than this one. We're going to live in the White House. I'm going to be the first lady . . . the first lady president. We're going to have three kids. Two boys and a girl. Or two girls and a boy. No, we're just going to have two kids—one boy and one girl. The boy's name is going to be Fred. And the girl's name is going to be Alexandria. I'm going to be the mother and he'll be the father. I can stay home and take care of the kids, while I'm president, because my office will be right in my house. I could get a maid to cook and clean, but on the weekends I'll plant a big flower garden, and take the kids to Disney Land, unless maybe I have to go to China or something—then maybe I could take them with me.

(*Picking up doll.*) This is my daughter now. Her name is Jesus Ann. She knows where God lives, too. Only Jesus Ann and me know. It's our secret. We got a master plan, her and me. We're going to get the guy who killed my father. See Jesus Ann's got magic powers and she can make us invisible so we can sneak into his jail cell and Jesus Ann will cast a really bad spell on him. She and me are going to make a big hole in him as if like he was shot—only from the inside out, so no one can tell it was us that did it, even if they get it on video-tape; so he bleeds and bleeds and really hurts, then he shrivels up and dies. Then he'll be sorry. Then maybe mom won't cry every night.

God said we could do it. He said it was O.K. because he deserves it because he's a bad man. And God knows. He knows everything.

Loreli

SAMANTHA GRACE KELLY

(A country girl from the deep South is checking the outcome of her home pregnancy test. After a frightened deliberation, she picks up the phone and dials a number she reads from the outside of the box.)

LORELI: Hi. I purchased this Response home pregnancy test, and it says on the box that you can call this number if you have any questions. Well, I followed the directions very carefully and, well, I know that, but I was just wondering how pink does it have to be? Because this is a very pale pink. Oh, I see. So it's definitely positive then? I'm positively pregnant. Well, isn't that wonderful. I can't wait to tell my husband the great news. Thank you so much. Bye.

Well Loreli, it looks like you are in deep doo doo.

Oh my God how could this happen to me again. I must be about as fertile as the Amazonian rain forest.

Oh baby why aren't you callin' me? I sure need to talk to you, now. You said you'd be back two days ago. You said you'd call me. I certainly hope you have a good excuse. I certainly hope your hands are tied—and I mean physically.

I hate when he goes off with those guys he works with. They're bad news. He's going to get himself into trouble hangin' out with them. I don't trust them one bit.

Charlie, why aren't you callin' me? I can't believe you aren't callin' me. If that phone doesn't ring within the next ten minutes I think I'm gonna die. I'm just going to shrivel up and die. And if I don't die, I'll kill myself. So help me God I will, Charlie. And my life will be on your hands then. Please call me. Please Charlie. Please.

He's gone off gettin' himself more drugs. I know it. I told him to stop with those drugs. Those damn evil drugs. I hate those drugs. He told me he stopped. I believed him . . . because he stopped hittin' me.

He only did it a few times. Always after bein' out drinkin' with the guys. He hurt me more inside than out. That's what he wanted, I think. 'Cause that's where he was hurtin'. I could understand that. I'd cry 'til I couldn't cry no more. It scared me somethin' awful. It was like he was possessed. I knew it wasn't really him that was hittin' me. I knew that. It wasn't Charlie. It was somethin' downright evil come over him. He couldn't help himself. It was those damn evil drugs and drinkin' is what it was. I told him so.

He was always sorry after he did it. One time he even cried. He told me that it was because he loved me so much that it made him crazy. He says we've passion between us, and sometimes it just explodes.

Charlie says I've got a fire in me. That's what attracted him to me. "Loreli," he says, "I believe you've got a fire inside you. I believe you are one red hot woman."

See, you gotta understand that as bad as Charlie can be, he's as good as he is bad. And I know he loves me.

Sometimes, I think Charlie's addicted to drugs . . . and I'm addicted to Charlie.

My Daddy was the same way, though. Same evil temper. He drank a lot. Finally killed him. All that drinkin'. Every once a week or so he'd come in yellin' at the top of his lungs about something or other. He never hit my mama. But he beat my brother Jimmy somethin' awful.

He never hit me. He called me his little princess. I remember when he used to sit me on his lap and say, "Princess, would you like some candy?" I never could wait for my Daddy to come home, and bring me some candy. 'Course it wasn't the same for Jimmy. I guess he must have dreaded the moment Daddy would walk through the door. He always found somethin' to yell at him about. And hit him. He hit him lots. I couldn't bear to listen to it. Jimmy would cry, and my Daddy would tell him that boys aren't supposed to cry. And I always thought my Daddy was right—that Jimmy shouldn't have cried. That he was just tryin' to teach him to be a man. But he shouldn't have hurt him like that. That's not right.

I'd always go into the kitchen with mama when it started. I was always thankful that I was a girl. I felt like I must be special since he didn't do that to me. Like I was the chosen one. I didn't have to go through that.

I've always had a thing about being the chosen one. Like God chose the Virgin Mary. Imagine bein' asked by God to have his baby. Hoowee. 'Course I guess she doesn't really have any choice in the matter. I mean, she couldn't exactly say no to God. I guess you can't have choices and be chosen both, maybe. That would be like havin' your cake and eatin' too, I guess. Well, I figure our fate's always in His hands anyway, no matter what we choose.

I remember when Charlie chose me. That was the most special night of my life. I had never met him before, but I'd heard about him because my friend Chrystal waitresses at the Windmill Restaurant, where he's a chef. I knew Chrystal had the hots for him. Well, he was just about the sexiest thing I ever saw walk through the door of The Bum Steer. Of course Bobby was flirtin' with me as usual that night. And Charlie just came right over, stood right in front of Bobby, came right in between us, looked me up and down and said, "You know, you've got the most beautiful eyes I've ever seen." Then he and Bobby started fightin' over me. You know how men are, so competitive. Of course, I *was* the prettiest girl there that night. I was wearin' my powder blue sweater. My mama always told me I looked best in blue. That's my good luck sweater. I always wear it on important occasions. It's real tight fittin'—but not low cut or anything—I wouldn't want to get a bad reputation.

Maybe Charlie'll want to marry me when he hears. Maybe he'll want to do right by me. Maybe he'll want me to have the baby. We could have a shotgun weddin'. Yeah, who am I kiddin', I'm sure he'd rather be killed by a shotgun than get married.

Charlie once said he thought I'd make a beautiful bride. He once told me that he thought I was pretty enough to be a model. "Loreli, you are so beautiful," he said, "You ought to be on the cover of one of them magazines." That's what he said.

I won't be no virgin bride, that's for sure. I'd have to have gotten married when I was fifteen for that. Yeah, I remember my first time. Jake was much older. But I told him I wasn't ready. One night we were at this party, and drinkin' every-thing under the sun. My head was spinning round and round, and Jake took me upstairs to this bedroom to lie down. Of course we started smoochin' once we got up there. Then I blacked out. The next thing I knew, Jake was on top of me. And I felt like a huge bomb just exploded in me. It didn't feel good, that's for sure. I couldn't exactly stop him at that point, though. I figured I asked for it, gettin' so drunk like that. I couldn't look at him, I was so disgusted with myself. Then I had this out-of-body experience. Because part of me had to get out of there. But part of me tried to pretend like I sort of enjoyed it. You know, so he wouldn't think I wasn't womanly or somethin'. I was afraid he might tell his friends that I was a cold fish or somethin', and I didn't want to get a bad reputation. (*Pause*) That night changed my life. Although I'm sure it meant nothin' to Jake. That was the night I became afraid of my own shadow. I was much stronger as a little girl than I am as a woman. I was never afraid of a thing. Never afraid to be alone.

I know I was askin' for it. Gettin' so drunk like that. I know Jake couldn't help it. Men can't control themselves sometimes.

One of my biggest fears in the whole world is getting raped. I think about it almost every day. Every time I'm by myself and I pass a strange man on the street, I think what if he's some kind of crazed lunatic and he's going to attack me out of the blue and tear off my clothes and ravage me. I have nightmares about it. Funny thing, you know? I believe I have nightmares and fantasies about the very same thing—bein' swept off my feet by some strange man. It seems to me like a woman's only power is her very weakness.

Sometimes I think that men are at the mercy of their you know what . . . and so are we. I mean they can't control it. It has a mind of its own. I read about it in this book, it's called their libido (*Pronounces it li-bye-do*). The thing that really scares me though is the thought of him losing his desire for me. Since it's not in his control, I think maybe one day he could just look at me, and all of a sudden feel nothin'. That's what really scares me.

When Charlie and I make love, I always wish that I could stop time. Right in the middle, you know what I mean? Stop it right then, somehow. Just say "now" and it would stop. And then I'd never be hungry, never feel naked again. Because we'd be connected, see? Like one being. Sometimes I wish I could swallow him whole. I just can't get close enough to him. I want to get inside his head. I don't know why. Just to know what it's like to be inside a life outside my own. But no matter how hard you try, you can't get inside another person's head.

Of course sometimes I hate sex. I do. Because sometimes there's just nothing spiritual about it at all. I'm a very spiritual person, see. There was a time when I actually thought about becoming a nun. I definitely don't have the right sort of habits for that.

One time when I was holdin' Charlie in my arms, I got this picture in my mind of him as a little baby at his mama's breast. I suddenly felt real angry and jealous of his mama. Crazy. See, he makes me crazy too. I wonder if he ever thinks about his mama. I mean it's not the same for a girl. We were never close like that to our Daddy.

You know, when I was a little girl I was a real tomboy. Hard to believe, I know. I used to play baseball, and climb trees. I never wanted to be like a girl. Because I liked boys. Always liked boys better than girls. And boys like me. (*Seductively*) Boy, do boys like me. Of course when I got older I realized that boys didn't like the girls who were like them anymore. That's when I changed. Because if you try to be like men, you ain't gonna be liked by men.

Please call, Charlie. God damn you. Why do you always disappear on me when I need you most? Please call me. Please don't break my heart again. You promised you'd never break my heart again. It still ain't completely healed from the last time. I'm too forgiving, I know. I can't help it. It's the weakness in me. He slaps me across the face and I hold him in my arms. He doesn't call me for three days, and I make him dinner. I'm either in love deep or I'm a glutton for punishment.

Maybe he'll want to marry me. Maybe he'll want to settle down and be a father. Maybe I won't have to go through that again. I think God could forgive me for doin' it once, but not twice. I know I'm no saint, God. But I'm not a whore either. Seems like a woman can either be one or the other. That's a hell of a choice, I think. What if you're somewhere in between? I'm not an evil person. I never hurt nobody. Please God, you've got to forgive me for this. Because you may be all I have.

Maybe Charlie'll tell me to have it. Maybe he won't make me go through that again.

I remember I went over to The Bum Steer. I said, "Mickey, give me something strong, and make it a double, I'm drinkin' for two." I was so scared to tell Kenny. But he was real good about it. He drove me all the way to that clinic, and even paid for part of it. We had to drive for almost three hours to get there. I was so scared. And it's not like you can pray for God to be by your side when you're doin' that. That's the real punishment of it. You just feel downright evil. That hurts even worse than the thing itself. I just kept telling myself that "It's not me going through this. It's somebody else. I don't know who. Somebody besides me." I remember Kenny bought me a chocolate milkshake after. Because I love chocolate milkshakes. I felt like I just had my whole inside vacuumed out. I just felt empty and dead.

I can't imagine what I would have done if I couldn't have had an abortion. I know some places it's illegal. I know it's a shameful thing. But I can't imagine what I would have done if I couldn't have done it. I was so young.

Some people say it's murder. Well, maybe it is. But it was inside *me*. Right? So that means it's part of myself that I killed, doesn't it? (*Looking at her stomach*) I mean it's right inside of you. It's not a life of its own. It's your life. It's my life. It's my life, and I will do what I damn well choose with it! You hear me, Charlie? I've made up my mind. This is my life. And I don't need you or anyone else to tell me what to do with it. This is my life. And I'm havin' your baby. And you can't stop me. No one can stop me!! How do you like them apples?!!

David's RedHaired Death

SHERRY KRAMER

(Jean has been talking to her good friend, Marilyn, about her brother, David. While Jean was driving to meet Marilyn, David fell from a burning hotel window and died.)

JEAN: A fall from a great height changes everything. Take a penny, for instance. If you drop it on the floor, you probably don't even bother picking it up. If you drop a penny from the top of the Empire State Building, however, that penny transforms itself into the weight of a thousand or more pounds on its way to the ground. Good luck picking it up then. On a good day, not too much wind, the penny will be embedded a good foot into the concrete, straight down. If you drop a woman from the top of the Empire State Building, she is transformed into that famous picture that appeared in *Look*. She is lovely, and young, and perfectly dressed in a trim suit. Her blond hair flows gently in waves that frame an angelic face. She lies on what looks to be a deep, soft, rich feather bed, an innocent, peaceful smile on her face, like an exhausted child who has succumbed to sleep the instant she hit the bed, too tired to pull the covers over her, too weary to squirm and disturb the perfect impression she has made on the satin coverlet—each line leading into the valley that cradles her body is clean, sharp, distinct. The photographer must have caught her in the instant after she lay down to sleep—in a moment, of course, the feather bed will flatten out, the satin—a dark, silky satin that shines where it catches the light—the satin will smooth out again, all the lines will be erased. But the caption under the picture reads: A TRAGIC SUICIDE. The soft, bright feather bed beneath the beautiful girl is in fact the crumpled roof of a Dodge. And they can carry the broken girl's body away, the photographer can take his prize and go on home. But the imprint of the body on the roof of the Dodge will remain.

I saw that picture for the first time in my pediatrician's waiting room. I was in for a polio booster, or a tetanus shot. I was eight or nine years old. Later the photograph turned up in a collection of *The Best from Look* that we kept on our coffee table. I could look at that picture for hours. She was so beautiful. She was as lovely as Snow White, as Sleeping Beauty—lovelier than both of them rolled together. But there was a catch. She would sleep, and there would be no prince. She was sleeping for no one. It would be forever wasted sleep.

I knew that she must have done it for love, but I was too young to really care. No, what bothered me was the Dodge. What I thought about while I looked at that picture was the moment after the picture was taken. When the owner of the Dodge returned.

I imagined the man, with his family—a family like our family, his nicely dressed wife, his three spoiled children, just down from a trip up the Empire State Building. The children are fighting about who will sit in the middle this time, I sat in the middle last time. Their father herds them along, he is in a hurry, worried about the meter. They have wasted too much time at the souvenir stand, parking tickets are expensive, do his children think money grows on trees? They round the corner, and come upon the place where they have parked their car. It takes several seconds for them to realize that they are looking at their Dodge.

And I wondered, too, just how romantic the photograph would have been if the family had not been at the souvenir stand so long. If they had been all loaded up and ready to go, the children squirming and elbowing each other in the backseat, their father checking a road map in the front. If they had come between a falling body and the ground.

The world is full of things that are falling.

From the Eczema Anthology

SARAH JANE LAPP

AMA: Whenever my parents mentioned intercourse at the dinner table, I always imagined genitalia in jars, floating in green formaldehyde. My first introduction to the male anatomy occurred before I could read, write my name, or ride a bicycle. The parents left town and sent me to daycare for an overnight weekend. I slept in a vast bed, curled to the side closest to the door. At some point, this door opened. The hall light entered the room and on its heels, the daycare lady's son, wearing only white Fruit-of-the-Looms. He sauntered over to my bed, towering. (*Beat*) The memory blurs. I cannot remember his face—did he have one? Did he have anything besides a torso—such as a heart or a brain? Doubtful. My head was at his waist. He reached into his underwear. *Do you know what this is?* Did I? *Do you want to touch it?* No. That I remember. No desire. No desire whatsoever. *Touch it.* Touch it? Touch *it?* Clearly, I knew "it" was not his thigh or his elbow—I needed no specific nomenclature. And he knew that.

Did he take it out? I do not think so. I refuse to remember. Did I touch it? I do not think so. *Touch it.* Why did I not? It. Do children not have more tactile fascination than most humans? A three-year-old not wanting to touch something! Ridiculous! When my niece asks to *see* my glasses, she wants to *hold* them between her fingers, though, clearly she is not myopic: she can see them just fine when they rest on my nose, a foot away. But to see *is* to touch.

Touch it. He must have taken IT out—otherwise, how else would he have expected hand contact? Touch it? That IT—that frightened—frightens—me the most. The ambiguity of the non-specific noun silenced me.

61

Alicia Maria Gets a Job at the Bakery

JOAN LIPKIN

I didn't always work at the bank. I used to work at the bakery. I had went to this bakery to buy bread. At this time, my English is not so good and I didn't know that supermarkets are for bread, bakeries are for birthday cakes. But no matter what language you speak, a big white cardboard sign in the window means maybe they are hiring. So I ask for a job. They say, do you have any experience in bakeries? I say, yes, I bake bread all the time. They say, no, do you have any experience *working* in a bakery? I say, no. They say, how about selling? I say, oh, yes! That is how I come to this country. On the boat. Selling. They say, no. Not *sailing*. *Selling*. To customers. By now, these two ladies, Astrid and Ingrid, are starting to cluck their tongues. They are clucking so loud, I almost look to see where the chickens are. And I am so hungry, I could eat the plastic models in the display case. I say, I know my English is not so good but I am going to night school to learn better. Maybe there are people who come in here whose English is also not so good so we speak the same language. They are not so sure. So I say, then put me in the back. I sweep the floors. You show me? I do it. Because I love bread. I eat so many sandwiches, I have a special feeling for this work. So Astrid says to Ingrid, or maybe it is Ingrid who says to Astrid, you know we are having a hard time getting someone for the graveyard shift. We could maybe try her out. And they hire me! Now I know why they are calling it the graveyard shift. Because it is killing me. I am also going to night school so I can speak better the English. By the time I get to the bakery, I am very tired and my head is full of the verbs.

But, Dios mio, I am happy. It is not much money, eh? But it is *something*, plus all the burnt bread and broken cookies I can eat! Instead of going hungry, my only worry is now the weight. Gracias el cielo! America is really something.

Excerpt from
Small Domestic Acts

JOAN LIPKIN

(Frankie is a butch lesbian in her thirties or older, responding
to charges from her lover that she doesn't talk enough.)

FRANKIE: I can't. I don't know why. And the more she wants me
to, the less I can. It's funny. I have so many conversations in
my head. But when it's time to open my mouth, the words
just leave me. I love Sheila. I love coming home, making love
to her, fixing things around the house. But it's not enough.
She wants more. She wants me to talk all the time and I just
don't know what to say. Maybe it's because she talks. Maybe I
want her to talk for me. Maybe it's because I live in my head.
I always did. I knew I was different. Found a place to go and
made it my own. But Sheila doesn't get that, see? And I don't
know how to tell her. Maybe I don't want to tell her. Maybe
she's right and I do want something that's just my own. I
don't really think anybody can understand another person,
anyway. At least, not the way it is for me. See, this is exactly
what I don't like. All this deep talk and thinking. It leads
nowhere. But Sheila wants words. Spoken *out loud* words.
And no matter what else I give her or do for her, it isn't
enough. She thinks I'm holding back. Maybe I am.
Sometimes, when we're lying in bed at night and I hear the
sound of her breathing, I start to choke. I look at her lying
next to me. I see the curve of her breast. This need rises up in
me so deep, I can't think where she begins and I leave off.
And then when she looks up at me with those big eyes, I can't
say anything. The air feels so heavy and moist with the scent

of her body and the smell of our sex. Sometimes, I envy Frank and Shelly asleep in their house, where the air is cool and thin. Each in their own separate world. Everything neat and clear.

Under Her Breath

FLORENCIA LOZANO

(The Talker, a bag lady, digs a half-eaten can of dog food out of her bag and using her fingers eats the remainders out of the can. She wears her clothes crazily, her overcoat wrapped around her head like a turban. Her underwear covers her face, crotch over her mouth. The Talker's story is set in a culture in which women no longer go to school. The only "mind-workers" are men.)

TALKER: There was w-man. She talk. She talk. In hills. In mountains. In trash cans. Behind bus station. McDaddy's. Every man know about she. They say she come screaming into world out of the cunt that way. Out of the slime. That way. She talk out of slit in her face and man say that 'cause the other slit don't work. Her slit workin' before she open eye to mama's black belly. Daddy slap mom tellin' her why doesn't the other slit work better. Figure he'll try it out. All the while he toppin' her she talk. Nearly died her, he slapped her hard. She go out searchin' life bags. Crust of donut. Stuck to Campbell's Soup cans she filled'r stomach. An' all time her slit be workin'. They could listen her from around the life bags workin' in her sleep. Throw stuff hopin' somethin' land in her slit. Choke on it? Nope. She got up. Still talkin'. Once nearly died . . . maybe couple onces. Reason: Couldn't eat. Spit up food out of slit. Talkin' stop her eatin'. *(She realizes that the can is totally empty. She begins to limp away.)* She survive. What she talk 'bout? Nothing. No things. No man stop. Listen. No man no. W-man know. W-man noisy cunt hide behind trash in schoolyard. Ugly face peepin' in them windows nearly died the mind-workers. Smear o' hot breath on window where she press edges of her crusty slit workin' always workin' scare the mind-workers all them men now. (*Breaks into song, tune of an alma mater*) Back to the good ol' days. (*Chuckle*) Yup, all them mind-workers now. Crazy! Crazy they call her—writing on the pissroom walls. They write she sucks cock on pissroom walls. She press her plugged up earhole 'gainst the window so hard it turn white. At that time mind-worker spot she. He see her earhole an' he let out yellin' they take she away NO MO' HIDIN' BEHIND TRASH the mind-workers run to the pissroom write on wall how crazy that bitch she suck my cock before class. (*Talker pauses and lets out a loud laugh*) They lyin' 'cause I know she can't do no cock suckin' she be talkin' all the way through. (*Laughs loudly*) Money make. She need money make. Rats nibble her fingers to the bone. W-man. Need money make. No place take w-man can't be hushin' her slit on the job. Clammin' it up. Need grub. Now. Can't even do the john business no john take her the way she talk. One time she need grub so bad she stuck sock in her mouth take a john. I hear it turn him on. Got to money make cleanin' pissrooms at eve hour when no one around. Hear the echo-co of her jabberin' through empty halls at eve hour. Spook me out. Well just forget it you think she got man and no screamin' little ones. You crazy want that. Nooo man want w-man, they don't want stuff no sock. Noooo. You crazy. Mister, she fearin' for her breath most of time. She try to live under her breath. Why? People want cut the bitch up. Cut, cut. Cut the clit I wonder if she talk so much. I hear 'em talkin'. Cut her nasty neck no sound come out no mo'. No sir, w-man on the run so many want to cut her up like chicken in the window. Even if she runnin' she talkin' under her breath.

LIVERPOOL JOHN MOORES UNIVERSITY
LEARNING SERVICES

Blue

MICHEL MAGEE

(*Becky is tidying the child's toys. She picks up a blue ball and hugs it to herself. She closes her eyes a beat and smiles. She begins in a straightforward manner.*)

BECKY: Right off I named her Blue seein' as she was born on the first night of the Blue Moon 'n all and bein' so little—shy a' three pounds, downright puny—cause a' comin' almost three months early 'n I didn't want her to go off havin' no name when they come for her by ambulance for the ride up to the hospital in Jeff City, right after Mama Linny and me baptized her and held hands and recited the Lord's Prayer with Nurse Carter aleadin', who is, I'll have you know, a direct descendant of Mother Maybelle herself. Doc Rhoads joined in for the "Amen!" (*Pause*) Then . . . Blue was gone.

(*Becky walks over to the porch steps, settles herself, and begins to snap string beans.*) When I recollect that night, I can still hear the siren wailin' down the highway with my baby, long past the distance an ear can take in sound for sure. Mama Linny, who is, for your information, my aunt what raised me up when my own good mama died birthin' me, says that kind of distance ain't measured in miles 'cause the heart don't know nothin' 'bout miles.

(*Becky pauses snapping the string beans, as though considering her next comment, perhaps for the first time.*) Hearts don't know nothin' 'bout speed either, if y'all's to ask me. It all a' got to goin' so *fast.* But when I play it over in my heart, that night moves like one a' them slowed down commercials for face soap or ice tea. (*Pause*) However, the truth be known here, Blue started a makin' her UN-hesitatin' way into this

68

world less'n two hours after I had ice cream with her daddy at the Tastee Top, just off the four-lane over by Bender's Dry Goods, where, by the way, I'd already started puttin' her layette away on lay away, in yella 'n white mostly, seein' as I didn't know if she was gonna turn out a boy or girl. (*Pause*) Ray—that's Blue's daddy—dropped me off to home early. We was in the very middle of another set-to over gettin' married, but the ice cream—or maybe it was the marshmalla butter-nutter toppin'—had me feelin' outta favor with my innards, so I let go a' my haranguin' and then sure 'nough, I started in with cramps 'n all and Mama Linny said she didn't feel it was a plain ol' bellyache from too much indulgence and we'd best call Doc Rhoads. And the rest y'all know.

(*She resumes snapping beans, shifting her position occasionally.*) Naturally right off, I called the hospital long distance up in Jeff City to inquire as to how Blue was gettin' on. The nurse said fine, and I said, well, if she's fine, then why's she there? (*Forcefully, in an I'm nobody's fool manner*) I didn't much care for the sassy answer she give back, so I packed my bag and never mind that I was practically *bleedin'* to death. I called Ray right now and told him he was a daddy—ready or not—and that he'd better do right by me and Blue and drive me up to where they was keepin' her and I wasn't takin' no for no answer, 'n *that* was *that*.

(*Snapping the bean she is holding with ferocity*) *Well!* Let me tell y'all . . . it's a good thing that child had her mama at hand, 'cause y'all never seen nothin' like it. When I got there they had tubes stickin' outta her pitiful little body and an IV *needle* in her head! (*Without a hint of condescension*) IV is for intravenous, I'll have you know. (*Tenderly*) Poor sweet Blue. Her little red baby arms weren't no bigger 'n my thumb. Veins too small. Thin as a *hayer* a nurse explained to me, so that's why they done it to her head where the veins is bigger. (*Becky turns to bring the laundry basket closer. Facing the audience, she drifts forward, absently touching the clothes still hanging on the line as she moves.*) 'Bout mid-point in our ordeal, I

also had me a serious talk with Blue. Not the out loud kind
. . . the kind you have in your head 'n the folks you're close
with pick up on. Now y'all take for instance my ol' Uncle
Sonny. He's got Alzheimer's 'n things mixed up but *good.*
(*Pause*) He'll say: "The WALLS is on fire! . . . And *who'r*
you?" (*With patience and sincerity*) And I'll say the walls ain't
on fire, ol' honey . . . 'n I'm *Becky,* same as you been seein'
ever' day a' my life. (*Pause*) Holdin' a conversation with Uncle
Sonny can wear a body thin. (*Pause*) But the point I was
makin' was there's time we'll be a'settin' quiet like . . . and I'll
be spinnin' in my own mind 'bout tryin' one a' them new
hybrid okras and Uncle Sonny'll come back from his private
wild blue yonder and say, "Yessum, okra'd be right fine". . . .
Like he was plugged into my head!

(*Becky starts to resume her position at the clothesline, but
pauses halfway. Almost absently, she touches the child's clothing
on the line. Her movements are slow as she begins to transform
her present reality to a particular moment in the Neo-natal
Intensive Care Unit. She will continue to touch an article of
child's clothing until the "break" to that moment is at hand.*)

I plugged into Blue's head that very same way . . . and I
got a sad, floatin' feelin' like Blue didn't know where she was
s'posed to be. Had things gone accordin' to plan, she'd a' been
safe and sound right inside me. But things didn't go accordin'
to plan—and here was my child, little as she was, weighin'
this mighty decision 'tween choosin' Earth or what surely
would be Heaven. So I said . . . (*The break with the present
occurs here, as she drifts center stage. The lighting dims until
Becky is spotlit on a darkened stage. Her hands are held to indicate they are resting on either side of an incubator. She begins
this passage as though speaking through her heart to Blue—slowly, and with great tenderness.*) listen here, Little Lady . . . this
here is your Mama a'talkin'. . . . You got to get better . . . and
bigger. There's a fine land outside these walls, Blue . . . and a
lake so wide you'll think it'll never end. . . . And at night . . .
there's stars . . . 'bout a forever's worth. . . . One of 'em

shinin' just for you. It's home. . . . (*Pause*) I know your early comin' was a surprise to you 'n me both, but there's such a thing as *nice* surprises. Just wait 'til you see all them pretty things I got put on layaway for you. . . . (*Long pause*) Blue, honey . . . I need to hold you, . . . and I can't if you gonna stay hangin' out on that ventilator, hole-up in your little Plexiglas box. Holdin's real good, Blue. 'Member that time . . . couple days back . . . I got to hold you seven . . . whole . . . minutes. (*Smiling, with tears about to spill*) They was the best seven minutes a' my life, Blue.

(*In pantomime, Becky opens an imaginary incubator and lifts out her baby. She cradles Blue in her arms. Her voice is barely above a whisper as she begins to croon.*) You are my sunshine . . . my only sunshine . . . you make me happy . . . when skies are gray. . . . You'll never know dear . . . How much I love you. . . .

(*Becky's voice breaks. Her expression is one of anguish as she looks up as though both pleading and praying.*) Please . . . oh, *please*, don't take my sunshine away. . . .

For Better or Worse

MADELEINE MARTIN

(The speaker uncorks a bottle of wine, takes a big gulp, and begins.)

But, Terry, you would not believe this wedding! I mean, here they are, on the banks of Rock Creek, with Jason and his sweetie Gretchen playing away on their little keyboards! And the music! Oh god! They were playing all this traditional holy-roller-Christian stuff along with "Here Comes the Bride" of all things. As if she had anywhere to come from! She was just standing there! But—now get a load of this—do you know what the guys were wearing? Her hubby-to-be, Rob—poor guy who knows not what he has gotten himself into—wore a white tux-coat with tails, cummerbund and all—but with jeans! No shit, jeans! With cowboy boots. I mean, give me a break. Pat's dress was just gorgeous. I will give her that. Brocade bodice with tons of beading and a big, full skirt. She really did look beautiful. (*Tears form in her eyes at the thought of it.*) But my God, Terry, the girl is nineteen years old! And get this—O.K.? One of her gifts was an iron, but it doesn't work, and the joke is, "Well, gee, Pat, is the iron turned on?" I mean, she knows nothing about cleaning or cooking . . . and here she is getting married! And they had bridesmaids and groomsmen—the whole nine yards. And I thought the whole time I was watching this, I thought—I'll give it two years tops! You *know*, I've thought about it, and I've thought if I ever got married—not that I would ever really get married—but I've thought that I'd just want the ceremony to be in a very small, very intimate chapel. I can see it in my mind's eye. It's white, with a huge steeple and sits on

72

several acres of rolling green grass. But up close, around the chapel—are carefully manicured gardens—rose gardens, mums—even herbs, all laced with tons of baby's breath. For a dress, I'd make my own, and it would be a suit with a fitted jacket and a fitted skirt. And it would be in the palest of sage . . . or perhaps a very pale salmon. In satin. With a tiny little Mandarin collar, and little buttons all down the front. . . . And I would have the shoes—three-inch heels—dyed to match. For flowers—my bouquet—I would carry a single red rose . . . maybe white. Who knows—black? *(She laughs)*

I can just see all the ladies wearing big hats and their men all decked out in their finest. And the cake would be spectacular too. I'd have one of those fountains between the two bottom layers of the cake and the top layer—but absolutely no bride and groom dolls on top. Oh, I have seen this cake top at a shop called "Your Special Day"—it's just down the street from my apartment in the city. And this topper is so gorgeous. It's two crystal bells tied together with a pink satin ribbon but I can order it with any color ribbon I need, and I'd want it to match my dress, so—either salmon or sage. And the mints will not be the cheap type of cream cheese and sugar crap that you press into the little molds a couple of days before the ceremony to save money! There's a confectionery right across the street from where I work. I love to wander through it on my lunch breaks, and they have the most wonderful mints. I would order their almond flavor, and a couple of the liqueur flavors. And my mixed nuts will be ALL mixed nuts with no peanuts.

(Quietly) I can just see it all so clearly. *(Quickly)* Not that I would ever consider getting married. But if I did—that's what it would be like.

Flux

SUSAN MILLER

(Jess is a college professor.)

JESS: I was a mommy once. You'll like this. I was a mommy
once. I held life and grew to immense proportions. I made a
baby come. I was so good and finally fertile with all of my
skin stretched as far as it would go. I worked hard at this baby
business. Vitamins and vegetables. I was a gracious hostess.
Gave the kid a good time. Held on tight. My little secret.
How will he get out, I thought? Oooh, that's scary. I won't
think about it anymore. So one night after a hearty meal, I
went to the hospital and started to have that pain women
have. Which makes you forget the room you decorated with
animals and the crib and the little undershirts. So this is what
women do, I said. Oh, I'm going to have to pay a lot more
attention to them from now on. They're quite a group. This
is no small thing, this baby operation. Who? Oh, yes. Baby.
My baby. The one I was waiting for, the one I was scared to
see. The one I actually loved before anyone said I could.
Here's how it's done. They pry your legs apart. They demand
your breath. They order you to push. To cease. And finally to
yield. There is a moment when you think everything will
come out of you. Then there is . . . there was for me . . . a
noise. I said, "What's that noise?" The man said, "It's a baby.
You have a son." Good. I love you little person. Now I'll
sleep. And they took him away. And they never brought him
back. The man came later with the other physicians and they
told me my son would probably die soon. And he did. And I
never saw him. Sure, I thought. Of course. How else could it
turn out. He was never really there. This is a lie, this baby

thing. I told those men to kindly leave and I fell asleep. There were flowers later and cards. All for the empty lady. (*Beat*) I wonder if he had any hair. (*Beat*) His crying sounded strange. I thought it was a noise.

Nasty Rumors and Final Remarks

SUSAN MILLER

(Max, a woman, talks to her lover, Raleigh, who is in a coma.)

MAX: The nurse said I could have a couple of words with you. I'll bet you just love that. Someone else giving me permission to come and go. Breaks every rule in the house, doesn't it? Listen, I can't find your Tiffany earrings anywhere. If I do, should I give them to Cat? Not that I've been very successful at finding Cat. But don't worry, she usually leaves some kind of trail. We're having a bitch of a time here with all your worldly goods, such as they are. I'm probably going to sell my car and buy yours from the kids. They could use the money. And besides, I like the way your car smells. As far as the taxes and bills and all that business shit, Nicky's got a good lawyer . . . except you did stuff the Sears bill between pages 104 and 105 of Tennessee Williams' *Collected Plays,* so God knows where the Department of Water and Power will show up. Now all of this is just in case. This does not mean you have to take it seriously. You can change your mind. I'll keep my crummy car. I'm only telling you these things so you won't be worried about details. But you can sit right up and shock the hell out of everyone, as far as I'm concerned. This place could use a little slap in the face, you know. Or . . . I mean, if that's too hard, right now, just move your index finger. Curse. Whatever. All miracles accepted. Shit, I believe in miracles. Clap your hands if you believe. . . . (*Pause*) This is terrific. I could sit here all day and talk, repeat all my old stories and you can't even tell me to shut up. Except you aren't laughing, and that's really what kept me talking all these years. (*Pause*) Actually, I'd love to hear you say SHUT UP. Go on, go ahead. Just for old time's sake. Give it to me good. C'mon. SHUT UP, MAX. Huh? How about it . . . please. Please tell me to shut the fuck up! (*Pause*) God, you're beautiful. You're not supposed to be that beautiful. This is intensive care, remember?

Scene of Shipwreck

PAMELA MILLS

(Margaret is a white South African, whose family is isolated on the veldt. Her unmarried daughter is pregnant and her married daughter has left her husband.)

MARGARET: What is this place? This place where the wind howls day and night . . . gently howls through the house as though in sympathy. I sit and watch the dust devils whirl red earth on hot afternoons which stretch out like the wired crosses that line the empty road and disappear in the haze. This is a lonely place. Sometimes when I'm rinsing my face in the basin and catch sight of myself suddenly in the mirror, I'm surprised. It is so white, my face. The skin feels too thin like that paper we used at school for maps. Black faces are so solid. They are darker than the earth, darker than the blood of mountains. They want nothing of one whose skin leaks out her soul. Damn them then. I don't care. Let the devil take them. Even though they surround me with smiles and gossip there is an ocean between us. They are not my friends. Oh God Oh God who can I trust, who can I count on? We came here, to the veldt, John and I, and there was nothing. We built this house, strong enough to keep out the wind, and then the shop, and we filled it and began to trade. Then we made the gardens and eventually the children and got the sheep. We were a family. But little by little that wind forced itself through and the holes grew, and the wind became everything. It took my husband, catching his hat and whipping it away, and then his trousers, flapping them wildly like loose sails until they flattened stiff and were stripped away. I tried to hold onto him, with both hands, but it was too strong, my hands got tired, I couldn't hold on anymore and I lost him. It was so sudden. I was unprepared. I'll manage without him then, I thought. I was young. I gritted my teeth. I had my children. Then one afternoon I heard a little sigh . . . go away, please go away. . . . But the sigh became a moan . . . be quiet! . . . and the moan . . . shut up! . . . became a keening . . . if I stick my fingers in my ears and talk very loudly I can't hear you I can't hear you I can't hear you! . . . until I thought . . . all I hear is the sound of my voice . . . I had gone mad. When I stopped there was silence. The last time was more playful, it rustled the papers and overturned the lamp. It was so infectious, I even caught its mood. . . . (*She begins to giggle as the wind begins to rise and objects are knocked over, making different sounds . . . and as the wind rises to a shriek, Margaret begins to laugh, a wild unrestrained laughter that reaches a pitch with the wind, and ends together with the wind, suddenly. Silence.*) I have nothing now. I feel the wind tear through my heart. What can I do? We are all strangers. All that holds us together is the wind.

Alabama Red Dirt

DIANNE MONROE

EVIE: The other day I got arrested. It wasn't something I was intending to do. It just happened. I hadn't been to a demonstration in I can't remember how many years. I don't really know what made me go to this particular one. But I did. And I got arrested. When my husband came down to bail me out, he was hollering about no wife of his was going to get herself arrested. Like I was the cop who arrested me. I hadn't really noticed it before. How he'd gotten that settled-in, middle-aged spread in body and mind. So we said we'd just grown apart. And I moved out. All civilized like. The only thing that makes me sad is little Melanie won't remember a time that her daddy lived with us.

People just aren't the same anymore. Maybe it's the air people breathe. All the pollution. Or the hole in the ozone. Or the chemicals in the food. Like at my job. They're all such *good* people. Recycle all their plastics and paper. Would never eat meat. *So concerned* about the planet. There's this little cafe where we sometimes go for lunch. Tables set outside under a striped awning. Last week there was this young woman on the corner begging. She had a little girl in a cardboard box. The child was neatly dressed and hugging a Raggedy Ann doll. I wanted to give her some money. But Nancy, that's my boss, said, "Don't you know they borrow those children from their friends, then take that money to buy crack cocaine?" So I kept my money and Nancy ordered the shrimp and crab salad and I ordered the vegetable plate and we talked about how the lumber industry in the Pacific Northwest was endangering the spotted owl.

Excerpt from
Giving Up the Ghost

CHERRIE MORAGA

(Marisa talks about her lover, Amalia, who has disappeared. As lights come up, she appears on her bed, rubbing her calves.)

MARISA: I woke up this morning the same way I have for
    months.
Sometimes I'm so mad, I can't even hear the birds
                                    outside my window.
I wake instead to this fluttering inside my chest
this heat
like the wings of birds are batting up a war dance
stomping out a fire in there.
(*pause*) I still wake up imagining touching her . . .
waiting to be touched.

(*pause*)
I must admit, I wanted to save her.
That's probably the whole truth of the story.
And the problem is . . . sometimes I actually believed
I could and *sometimes* she did, too.
She'd look at me that way, you know, with hope
in her eyes and it would light up her whole face
  . . . especially when we made love.
Sometimes that look would make me very nervous
but usually I tried to look past it
tried to get to the heart of the matter
of what we were doing and not get all locked up

thinking about what we were doing.
Thinking always made me nervous and her scared.

When she wasn't thinking, she'd come to me,
I swear, like heat on wheels!
I'd open the door and find her there, wet
from the outta-nowhere June rains
and without her even opening her mouth
I knew what she had come for.

I never knew when to expect her this way
just like the rains
never ever when *I* wanted it asked for it begged for it
only when *she* decided.

But she would lay herself down and wide open for me
like no woman I'd ever had before.
I think it was in the quality of her skin.
Some people, you know, their skin is like a covering.
They're supposed to be showing you something
when the clothes fall into a heap around your four ankles,
but nothing is lost . . . you know what I mean?
They just don' give up nuthin.
Pero Amalia . . . Eeeholay!

She was never fully naked in front of me,
always had to keep some piece of clothing on . . .
a shirt or something always wrapped up around her throat,
her arms all outta it and flying . . .
but she'd never want it all the way off.

What she did reveal, however . . .
each item of clothing removed was a gift,
I swear, a small offering
a *suggestion* of all
that could be lost and found in our making love

together.
It was like she was saying to me,
"I'll lay down my underslip, mi amor . . .
¿Y tú? ¿Qué me vas a dar?"
and I'd give her the palm of my hand to warm
the spot she had just exposed.

Everything was a risk.
Everything took time . . . was slow
and painstaking.

I'll never forget after the first time we made love
I felt . . . mucho orgullo y todo de eso . . . like a good lover
and she says to me . . .

"You make love to me like worship."

And I nearly died, it was so powerful
what she was saying.
And I wanted to say but didn't . . .
"Sí. La mujer es mi religión."
(to herself) If only the sex coulda saved us.

You know sometimes when me and her was
                                            in the middle of it,
making love . . . I'd look up at her face, kinda grey
from being indoors so much in that cave of a house
                                            she lived in.
But when we were together, I'd see it change, turn
this real deep color of brown and olive
like she was cookin inside . . .
(remembering) tan linda.
Kind. Very very very kind to me to herself
                                            to the pinche planet
and I'd watch it move from outside the house
where that crazy espíritu of hers had been out makin tracks.

I'd watch it come inside through the door
watch it travel all through her own private miseries
and settle itself finally right there in the room with us.
This bed. *(she pounds it)*
This fucking dreary season.
This cement city.
With us.
With me.
No part of her begging to get outta this.
Have it over. Forget.

And I could feel all the parts of her move into operation.
Waiting. Held. Suspended.
Praying for me to put my mouth to her
and I knew she knew we would find her como fuego
hot hot hot mojada mi mujer
and she could be mi muchachita y mi mujer
en el mismo momento
and just as I pressed my mouth to her, I'd think . . .
I could save your life.

It's not often you get to see people that way
in all their puss and glory
and *still* love them.
It makes you feel so good,
like your hands are weapons of war
and as they move up into el córazon de esta mujer
you are making her body remember
it didn't hafta be that hurt, ¿me entiendes?
It was not natural or right
that she got beat down so damn hard
and that all those crimes had *nothing* to do
with the girl she once was two, three, four
decades ago.

It's like making familia from scratch
each time all over again . . . with strangers
if I must.
If I must, I will.

I am preparing myself for the worst,
so I cling to her in my heart,
my daydream with pencil in my mouth,
when I put my fingers
to my own
forgotten places.

Florence Commuter Airlines

LAVONNE MUELLER

(Florence may be a young, hot-shot pilot or an old-timer who has seen it all and has come up the hard way. Florence is in her office, staring out the window. A picture of her mother hangs on the wall.).

FLORENCE: (*A beat as she stares out the window. Then she goes to the door, opens it, and calls out.*) Hot chocolate, Doris. (*She goes back to the window, leaving the door open. She is happy as she looks out at the bad weather*) We're going to pitch like a circus tent in a windstorm. (*A beat as she listens. Doris is typing offstage through the door, and Florence is talking to her.*) What? Don't tell me this is gonna blow over. I hate a pessimist. Just get me some hot chocolate, Doris. (*Beat*) Cholesterol? When have I ever cared about cholesterol? (*Looking out the window, with self-pity.*) I got up this morning happy. I said to myself—Florence, you're going to take yourself a 200-mile-an-hour sled down a slope of black snow. Now . . . there's some clearing to the north. You know what the passengers are like when it's clear, Doris? (*A beat as she listens to Doris' typing through the door.*) They want me to call out when we're going over Lord and Taylor's like a bus driver. (*Beat*) Ahhhhh, it's getting darker. Nice wall of festering goop to the west. Stalactites of muck. Froth. Sludge. (*Calls to open door*) Doris, haven't you finished our flight plan yet? (*Computer typing is heard for an answer as Florence goes back to studying the weather outside the window*)

Weather was about like it is now when I landed on the expressway last week. Just . . . coasted her with the flaps down. Lowered the gear. Hit the expressway with the wheels tearing off. Belly of the plane breaking apart sweet like tinfoil around a Thanksgiving turkey. Now that's friction, Doris. Digging up the asphalt like a giant plow. I flattened a Cutlass Supreme . . . slid its bucket seats down the pavement at a hundred miles an hour. FAA don't even slap my hands. (*Florence goes to the door.*) It's about time to fill her up, Doris. (*Beat*) And get my hot chocolate on the way back. With marshmallows. (*Typing stops.*)

What? My Mom called? Why didn't you tell me right away! (*Beat*) I know . . . I know . . . our flight plan. (*Beat*) Mom said . . . what? (*Beat*) She's . . . She's . . . my mother is going to fly Florence Commuter Airlines sometime today? To visit family? (*Beat*) Which family? Which flight? (*Beat*) Whattaya mean she wouldn't tell you. She . . . doesn't want to make . . . any of the girls nervous! She just wants us to know she believes in us! (*Beat*) My mother is terrified of flying. She always takes the Greyhound. Why is she doing this to me now? (*Beat*) She saw an old Amelia Earhart movie. (*Beat*)

Doris, don't sit out there and tell me my mother is flying our airline today. (*Beat*) Under a false name? (*Beat*) Right . . . right . . . so none of the girls are nervous. (*Beat*) Doris . . . wait. After you gas up, bring me back a Sanka. Black. (*Beat*) I know I don't drink Sanka. But I'm not going to die up there from clogged arteries. Not now. Not when Mom could be on my plane.

I know she's not going to be on *my* plane. Don't be so literal. She'll be in *my* airline. In *my* sky. (*Florence goes to the window to study the weather.*) Some of those black cloud-tops out there are probably up to 53,000 feet. (*Beat*) Carla will be doing her usual banking in the headwinds—bending the old plane like a bronco buster. And Janice—she'll be up to her near-misses on Loons, Piper Cubs, low cruising pigeons.

(*Florence goes to the intercom and switches it on.*) Hangar? Kate, I want you to find me a flashlight. (*Beat*) You put one in my file cabinet? Hold on. (*Florence goes to the file cabinet and fingers through the files and can't find it. She goes back to the intercom.*) Not there. (*Beat*) Filed under . . . *what?* (*Florence goes back to the file cabinet. She reads the file titles aloud as she fingers the files.*) Feverjets . . . figbolts . . . fillings. (*She pulls out a flashlight. She goes back to the intercom.*) Today . . . we are not going to use this flashlight to look in our mouth for any lost fillings or loose crowns or chipped back teeth. Today, we're each getting a flashlight and dropping to our knees to check the undercarriage of our plane. Before we take off. That means—all five pilots and all five flight engineers in Florence Commuter Airlines. (*Beat*) Are my pilots and crew in the hangar . . . ready for today's briefing? (*Beat*) Good. Turn on the squawk-box.

(*Florence picks up a microphone on her desk and speaks into it.*) Women, this is Captain Florence. With the morning briefing. (*Beat*) I want to tell you all I'm real proud of last week's "on-time arrivals." We're way ahead of any other commuter airline. We've left all the macho-dudes in the dust. And that's what flying's all about—I don't care how many alternative airports you landed at or what holding pattern you cannonballed through. (*Beat*)

Now today, women, I'm asking you all to fly S-O-P. Standard Operational Procedure. I know a lot of you find the Flight Manual reactionary. I know we gotta go one better than the Manual. We're women. But today, all of us are going back to the Book. That's an order. (*Beat*)

Now, some of you are going to test me. I'm telling you— don't. You'll want to shut down an engine over Iowa City, maybe. Advance the three-throttles with your feet. Land in a pasture for some organic yogurt. Do it tomorrow. Next week. 'Cause you're not going to do it today. (*Beat*) Men fly normal. All the time. Just shows how easy it is. (*Beat*) This company is democratic. Seniority is the basis for promotion. That's why I'm here. And that's why you're there. (*Beat*) I don't have to tell you I grew up at the airplane fence. I've been flying since I was nine. My first solo was like my first kiss. Took me out across pea patches and cornfields in a rig I built myself out of orange crates and my sister's roller skates. Used to get airsick so I flew with a bucket between my legs. In high school, I asked for the old man's plane the way other kids asked to use the car. *(Beat)*

Now, I know that what I'm asking you to do today is not cool. I'm not advocating anything sexist. I like to fly "homing pigeon" just like the rest of you—no radar, no visibility, no ground flares . . . diving at the runway, or landing in a mall to check out the college guys. Look, I understand how you feel. But today, it's dress code all the way. That means—no surf skirts, no Guns 'n Roses tank tops, no shoulder chains or metallic boat cloaks. *(Beat)* When you're nose to rear burning fuel on the taxiway waiting to depart today, you remember that sometimes we gotta grit our teeth when the Company asks us to. That means no flying on the edge of a stall. No . . . Square Loops, Double Snap Rolls during takeoff. I like a good "tail slide" . . . put the plane backwards for a while before nosing over. A few Hammerheads and Vertical Climbs by Moline's McDonald's. Who doesn't? I'm the one who took the first Florence-Commuter in a loop-marathon. Sixty-four consecutive spins carrying 15 tourists over Sandwich, Illinois. So don't tell me what you're giving up. O.K.? *(Beat)*

I'm not asking you to do something I'm not going to do. I got my manual right here. And I'll see you in the troposphere. Have a good flight. *(Florence puts the mike down and switches off the squawk-box. She picks up the flashlight from her desk. Florence turns off the office light, turns on her flashlight and exits through the door. She slams the door roughly causing the picture of her Mom to fall to the floor.)*

A Drink After the Storm

LAVONNE MUELLER

(Olive Wiggins, a 19-year-old girl in Army fatigues, comes in to a coffee shop and sits down. Corporal's stripes are on the shoulder of her fatigues, and a high-impact magic marker hangs from her dog tags.)

OLIVE: *(To an unseen waiter)* Coffee. With cream. *(Slaps money on the counter)* Yah . . . yah, I was in Saudi. *(She drinks.)* What? Sure I'm a real corporal. You're not the only one to ask me that. A lot of people want to know what it's like being a woman soldier. Are you a token, they ask? A puppet? A crumb thrown in the mouth of war? Well, I'm as much a warrior as Ike . . . Westmoreland . . . Schwarzkopf . . . or any of the others. *(She salutes the waiter. She holds the salute.)* The name's Corporal Olive . . . Olive for peace, Wiggins. *(She drops the salute.)* I used to date some Arab from Paw Paw, Illinois, before the war. Bahiaddin Ali Faris Ketsaraa Abdul Chucheep. I called him Dul for short. He worked in a Taco Bell at the I-94 Truck Plaza and he always gave me free coffee even before we started going out. Dul was really nice for an Arab. He didn't wear a dish rag with tassels on his head or do chants from one of them parachute towers. You know, pretty ordinary. He did have a "prayer bump" just below his hairline from pressing his forehead to the ground in pious meditation. I got him to wear his bushy eyebrows combed up over it so nobody could really tell. And occasionally I'd get aggravated with the "Mecca indicator" on the ceiling of his Honda. We'd go for a simple drive in the country . . . and this fancy compass gadget kept reminding us which way to bow our heads in prayer when Dul didn't even have automatic shift.

Dul was sweet, though. He gave me a tape of Bluegrass II for my birthday. With the war and all, he's not at Taco Bell anymore and I wouldn't wanna get it on with him now, anyway. But sometimes when I was walking in the Kurdistan mountains dodging our own A-V8 jump jets or in the desert with a full moon out feeling lonely with only camels and cute little oil-slicked cormorants, I'd think of him.

I was proud to be in Saudi on the historic day the war started. I was PX Supply Clerk at the time. It was my job to help our Saudi allies understand instructions on various boxes and jars of stuff given out freely by Special Services. I didn't speak Arabic, of course. And none of them Gulfies spoke English. But it was my lucky break to act-out how to use a hemorrhoid suppository for a member of the Afghan Mujahedeen. I want to tell you that Afghan was so grateful he gave me the helmet of a dead Colonel from the Republican Guard. I got it hanging up under my Elk's head in my kitchen in Shabonna.

This high-impact magic-marker I wear around my neck was used for bomb-signing. The men wrote their thing on a bomb or missile, whatever, and then their personalized weapon was forklifted across a pontoon bridge to me in a quonset at the Port of Jubail. "Cram-it Sad-dam it." Stuff like that. I went over each word carefully in permanent black. Then I signed my own name like the famous painter Norman Rockwell. It was very spiritual to think of my "name" maybe slamming into Tikrit, Hussein's home town, and his forty wives diving under a prayer mat for cover. You know, like *them* blasting Kennebunkport.

Don't think I was in the rear. I want you to understand there were a lot of missiles and 50-caliber tracers around me all the time. Of course no real people got wasted. Just . . . Sheiks, bedouins, Ottomans . . . stuff like that. It got kind of bloody sometimes. I've seen a lot of death. And I want to tell you, the Iraqi give off the yip of a dying dog. Death for a pagan is not quiet.

Well, I gotta get up early. I'm being air-lifted to the Strait of Hormuz tomorrow. To a huge desalting plant. The Army feels all that discarded salt can be stockpiled in case we go to war with another one of them Mesopotamian countries. Putting salt back in the enemy's drinking water is okay by the Geneva Convention.

I'll probably be back in Illinois in a year or so. No doubt you'll see me driving around DeKalb County in one of my Humvees. Thank god around here you can always pull any time into a station for gas as nobody in this country closes in the middle of the day for prayer. (*A beat as she responds to the waiter*) Oh, I'll be glad to give you an autograph. It'll be fun to sign a napkin for a change. I'll even use my bomb-marker. (*Saying as she signs*) Corporal . . . Olive . . . Olive for peace Wiggins. (*Hands napkin to the waiter and exits.*)

Separations

JANET NEIPRIS

(Heather, a young mother, is speaking at her infant daughter's funeral.)

HEATHER: It was a very old hotplate. It had been lying around the attic for years, my mother-in-law tells me. The cord must have been frayed. But no one noticed. We're looking into these matters because we're trying to determine the nature of the accident. Ordinarily I'm a fairly careful person, in control. (*Pause*) But I wanted to make a nice dinner, like a family. I made lamb curry with raisins—yellow raisins. It happened in a second, like an explosion. I tried to get to the crib where it caught fire. You couldn't. A human being couldn't. It was like . . . the atomic bomb. I screamed down into the street. People just kept walking by. Not a lot of people. It's the suburbs, you know. The houses are far apart. But people . . . I saw them, walking their dogs, jogging . . . I screamed so loud I thought I'd burst . . . blood, dripping down my legs . . . I could feel it. I didn't know that could happen to a woman, that you could make it happen. . . . For months, I'd had this dream, that I'm sitting by a pond in the sun, yellow tulips by the pond . . . blowing. . . . I am sitting under an oak tree. Suddenly, from out of the water comes a large black swan, walking towards me, across the grass, he has a red beak. He comes to where I sit and starts to peck at my shoulder. I am wearing a thin lavender blouse. . . . The swan continues to peck. Good God, I think, doesn't anyone see? People can see. They have time to see. . . . The baby never made a sound. So quiet. Just lay there. I grabbed her and I held her and I screamed so loud, I'm telling you. . . . No one answered. (*Pause*) I was a good girl. I was as good as gold.

Emily

JANET OVERMYER

(Emily enters with a birthday candle set in a cupcake. She sets it down and lights it.)

EMILY: I wrote my parents—inspired by a book—I wrote them that I loved them and forgave them. And for the moment, I suppose I did. My mother wrote back that she didn't understand about forgiving. My father didn't reply at all. My mother had an okay funeral for him with his American Legion buddies attending, and the stories they told! So funny, so considerate, such a good friend. Not the man I'd lived with at all, not at all. If I'd walked into that funeral without knowing, I never would have guessed whom it was for. But, you see, I was the only one in that room who knew what it was like to be his daughter. House devil, street angel. Aren't we all? But to that extent?

My mother, now. That was a difficult story. She started to become senile after her husband, her antagonist, died. She needed the fighting, it seems. She began begging the neighbors for food even though I went over once a week with eggs and milk and soup and frozen dinners. People complained, and she had no relatives apart from me. I thought of moving her in with me, but I had to go to work. She couldn't have stayed here alone. I have a house now, did I tell you? She could hardly see or hear and I couldn't leave her alone all day. And a sitter, even if I could have found one, would have cost my whole pay. So—I had to put her into a nursing home. Once, when she was in her fifties, fat and healthy, she said, "EmilyYvonne, promise you won't put me in a home." And I promised. It was easy then. I hated to do it. I did, I really did.

But you can see there was no choice, can't you? I couldn't do anything else. I had to see that she was taken care of. I did the best thing, the only thing. I did, I did. I DID! (*Pause*)

When Seawhiskers died I went into hysterics, couldn't eat for a week, taught my classes in a stupor. "You loved that cat too much," my mother kindly explained; her idea of consolation. When my parents died, I couldn't squeeze out one tear. Well, all right, maybe just a few for my mother—but none for my father. They had died years ago, in a way, when I needed them and they weren't there emotionally for me. When their encouragement might have made all the difference. But no grief at all for their deaths. That's unnatural, isn't it? Maybe I am their bad little girl after all.

Pocket

KATY PETTY

Look, I really don't want to talk about this—I'll see you later.

(*Gets up to go. Turns back in response.*) I *know* I'm a bitch—I'm a "bitch"—but what am I going to do? I just don't like him anymore.

I don't know what happened—the same thing that always does. Ugghh.

You know, sometimes I wish that I could use my vagina as a pocket. It would be so much more practical that way. I'd probably get a lot more use out of it, too. No, you know what I mean—I'm always losing things and forgetting things, what if I could just shove 'em on up there and keep them inside me.

Yeah! Pandora had her "box," right?

I mean, my uterus is empty *(Knocks on wood),* why can't I use it for personal storage? Like the secret hiding place behind the bookshelf. And each month, instead of leaking icky blood and membrane and goop—I would leak knick-knacks and memories. Things that I had forgotten that I had in me. It would be five days of gifts and surprises, not five days of mess.

I'd be a pocket—full of dreams and memories and ideas. I'd be a piñata (*Adopts a "flamenco" pose and Spanish accent*), bursting once a month, and little presents would fall right into my lap. Regalos from me—to me.

And anything that I didn't want out I could put right back in because it's safe inside my pocket. It's only safe inside me.

Robin

ANNE PHELAN

ROBIN: People always make fun of L.A. Especially if they're from the eastern seaboard. They seem to think the whole country stops once you get west of Philadelphia. Of course, if they're looking to make a buck and get famous, L.A. is the only way to be. C'mon, we all watch TV. At one time or another, we've all succumbed to the temptation of at least starting the *TV Guide* crossword puzzle. But New Yorkers? Forget it! They think that enduring the constant humiliations and danger of their city makes them urban pioneers. They go on about how the City of Angels has no seasons. Ninety-five percent of the people in New York wouldn't know what season it was if they didn't pass Central Park in a taxi once in a while. Trees? What's trees to a New Yorker? You can't even tell you're on an island, unless you commute by car from the burbs. The rest of the people in this country know what a tree is. The smuggest expression I know is on the face of the hopelessly parochial New Yorker who says, with an irrepressible arch of the eyebrow, "Well, I don't drive." Like they were saying, "I don't smoke." At least in California you don't have to go twelve rounds every day to prove to yourself you're still alive.

My parents were divorced seven years ago. God knows they had problems. Both of them. I don't think they're significantly happier apart—more like it's one less problem. My dad drinks and screws around. My mother was ruined by an education courtesy of the Sisters of the Sacred Heart of Jesus. They call them the "Madames." But not because they're hookers. They prepared Mom for a life in eighteenth-century France, but not Rodeo Drive. She's still trying to get herself into 1900. When I started working for Dad, she wasn't real thrilled about it. Not that she'd ever say anything. My mother has never articulated a strong opinion about anything in her life. It's all innuendo. The television studio was a real rush for me at the beginning. It got routine after the first year, but I still get a little lightheaded sometimes. People feel they have to be nice—the other producers and writers. They say things like "You've got a great future ahead of you, Robin, baby. You've really got it. You could be another Sid Perelman!" The fuck I am. I was raised on sitcoms—grew up in front of the television set. Picked up some from my Dad. I've reached the height of my potential and I'm twenty-eight years old. If the market keeps expanding, I should always be able to earn a living. I wish to Christ I was an underachiever. That I had the talent I'd sold out to regain. Because I look at the ones who do waste themselves and I could cry. I'll hit seventy and have my retrospective at the Museum of Broadcasting and all there will be are one hundred half hours of "Molly and Marty" episodes. At least "Bullwinkle the Moose" was intelligent. I'm between lovers at the moment, that's why I'm a little down. I keep winding up on blind dates with foreigners, most of whom can't hold their liquor. They also all regard anything that lasts more than two weeks as tantamount to a marriage proposal. Marriage! Christ, can you believe there are still people who still get married, even with community property laws the way they are. When I was in high school I swore I'd never get married. Not after watching my parents. Then I found two couples who looked happy. One of them is divorced now, and the other . . . Jenny pretends Chris isn't screwing half the world, and Chris proceeds to do exactly that. There isn't one friend of ours, male or female, he hasn't come on to. Including me. Maybe there are lots of happy, eminently fulfilled, loving, caring married people. They must all live in a very small town in Montana.

There's this thing that happens to me after I've been seeing a man for a while. If I really play hard to get, it happens after I've slept with them once. Twice, at most. I call it the "jerk factor." Usually after the first three months you tell yourself that something is not quite right. But they're so cute when they smile or so good in bed you tell yourself that nobody's perfect and just go on with it. But something about them . . . the way they treat you, or how you feel when they call—and God knows, how you feel when they say they'll call and don't—you start feeling kinda silly. Not silly-happy. Silly-foolish. I mean, you think you're the biggest jerk ever to come down the pike simply for taking them at their word. The longer it goes on, the more they seem to do it on purpose, with real malice aforethought. Every waking moment of theirs is spent thinking of ways to reduce you to this jerk-dom. And I can never see why. I just risk a massive coronary every time the phone rings. There is no time limit on the jerk factor. I have guys that I used to go out with and haven't seen in years who call once every six months and leave me drowning in a pool of it. You see, this state is not a criticism of your body or how well your perm came out or whether or not you're nice to your mother. It has nothing to do with your intelligence quotient. Or even the kind of Trivial Pursuit type of mind I've got. I can even remember the entire menu at my birthday party in 1965—I was five. Creamed chicken, Birdseye frozen peas, tomato aspic, milk, and a Duncan Hines cake—chocolate, with Betty Crocker chocolate frosting.

The only time I was not a victim of the jerk factor was with the guy I dated in college—Jamie. He was okay. Not great in the brains department, not ready for the Albert Schweitzer award, but better than most. We did have fun, sometimes. And we had great sex. Often. After every meal, practically. After the first three months I realized that whenever we attempted any sort of intellectual conversation, I spent more time defining any word of more than three syllables than anything else. Jamie's contributions to these conversations consisted of, "Honey, what do you mean?" and "Gee, honey, that's really neat." I routed the jerk factor very simply. By cheating on him every chance I got. I had a serious affair with a passionate young painter the summer Jamie spent in Boston tutoring dumb rich kids at a prep school, and then I decided to get self-righteous. I told Jamie about the painter. He was beside himself. Went on a drinking binge. He'd have these crying jags where he'd sob for so long I'd think he was choking to death. He did even more drugs than usual. Eventually we got back together. The painter relegated me to jerk heaven. Jamie and I broke up six more times, until we both got so bored we gave up.

I remember Jamie's face the day I met him: this angelic smile and huge blue eyes, full of trust. I saved myself from the jerk factor, and took that look out of his eyes for good. His mother was ready to kill me for what I did to her baby. Bad enough I took his physical virginity. If I ever beat the jerk factor again, I'll either marry the bastard or shoot myself. I talked to Jamie a few weeks ago. He's been dating this nurse for a few months. And he's starting to do to the nurse what I did to him. The guilt hasn't caught up with him yet, but it will. Even he can't beat the system.

Snake

SHARON HOUCK ROSS

(Anne, a middle-aged woman wearing a hospital gown and a flamboyant scarf around her neck, is preparing to leave. As she speaks, she takes items of clothing out of the paper bags they've been packed in and layers them on over the gown.)

ANNE: Take either bed. I'm on my way out the door.

They'll be after your dreams in here, you know. Get ready. Once they have your scent, they'll chase you till you drop. Round and round. Took me six months to get smart enough to just . . . stand . . . still.

Mine were about snakes. They had themselves a text-book field day with that one. Snake: evil, right? Danger, deception, penis. Put the Bible with Freud and you have an image of remarkable terror. They had me scream-dreaming snakes every night of my life . . . until I stopped sleeping. I kept setting and resetting this little timer on my watch. But they caught me and made me sleep. They can do that in here, you know. Oh, yeah, they can do a lot of things they shouldn't.

But after a while at night, I got used to Snake, my smooth soft sun Snake. And you want to known something? She didn't look a thing like Freud's penis. Female. Pregnant. Yeah, we talked.

"Listen girl," she said. "There were lots of things running around in that garden that got too big for their britches. All I did was to even up the sides. Equal access to the big tree. Knowledge leads to Truth and the Truth shall set you free, right? I just wanted a fair game."

Then she pulled herself high into the air and got real still.

"Come on over here," she whispered. "Look me right in the eye. What you see?"

"Just me. I see my self, is all."

"Yeah? Now look up there to the heavens. What you see?"

"Air. Nothing but air."

"Bingo," she said.

And that's when I started remembering the dreams I'd had before my little "episode." A real breakthrough, see, because my memory tends to come and go. And then I knew. I knew again what I used to know. Oh, yes. Snake had been whis-hisspering to me all along, but I was too scared to listen.

Had my own little garden all fenced in, see. We're talking husband, three children, house on an acre, two cars, four dogs, three hamsters, and a rabbit. We're talking the American happy ever after dream deluxe. We're talking a woman who one day after lunch took her best butcher knife and sawed into the jugular on the left side of her neck.

So they tell me. *(Lifting her scarf)* And they point to the scar to prove it. See, the "treatments" took things from me. It was like lightning zigzagging through my head. And now, inside, there are all these little pieces of memory, always tumbling into different patterns that don't quite fit.

I should've listened to Snake.

I hope they don't do that to you. (*The newcomer is crying.*) Oh, here now, I've done it, haven't I? I'm sorry. Look, don't worry. You're in much better shape than I was at first. At least you're sitting up. And both your jugulars still connect your head to your shoulders, right? But you know what? (*Rummaging through the bags*) I'm going to leave something with you. For luck. I want you to have it.

See, the last summer that I can remember, I went to Rome. And in one of the museums, I saw this statue of an ancient goddess. She . . . drew me. Oh, yes. She stood there before me with arms outstretched, and in each hand, you

know what she was holding? A sheaf of wheat, flowers . . .
and a snake.

Here are the first two.

The snake you'll find for yourself.

(*Anne exits carrying the rest of her possessions in a paper
bag.*)

LIVERPOOL JOHN MOORES UNIVERSITY
Aldham Robarts L.R.C.
TEL. 051 231 3701/3634

Stupid People

TAMMY RYAN

(A woman emerges out of the darkness; she is impeccably dressed in a tailored navy suit, matching pumps. Her hair falls down around her face, out of a loosening bun. She tries to pat her hair back into order as she talks.)

There are certain signs people wear on their lapels that say: this person is sensitive or dangerous, don't push them. This person doesn't laugh at Polish jokes because—guess what? She's Polish! God, I can't tolerate a stupid person.

I grew up in a large working-class family full of stupid people. Don't get me wrong, I loved them and all, but they lacked a certain—I don't know, beyond class—they lacked foresight. An ability to know which way the wind will blow. My sisters, God bless them, didn't have half a brain between them. Both married young, stupid husbands, do everything for them, then when the man inevitably walked out the door neither one of them could pay a gas bill. Well, I was the baby. They'd tease me, I was adopted. I'd cry, put on a good show, and pray it was true.

Oh no, don't get that idea. I hate when people blame their adult lives on unhappy childhoods. Outside of their stupidity I had quite a happy childhood. Look at my brother! He's a lawyer, happily married to, of course, a lovely woman, three wonderful, healthy, happy children—oh, he's got it all. Well, it's that male/female double standard thing. I knew right from the start I wouldn't have gotten here today if I'd gotten married. All right, I don't want to sound bitter! I just realized young that I had several strikes against me: I came from poor, stupid people, and I was female. I'd have to work twice as hard as everyone else, for half the results. (*Leans against chair, slips off shoe, rubs her foot.*)

When I got out of college, every employment agency I went to wanted to give me a typing test. I had a degree, I told them. That's why I went to college, so someone else could do the typing. I asked the last counselor, a woman no less, if a man with a college education came looking for a job, would he have to take the typing test? "Oh, no!" she said, thinking I had a boyfriend looking for a job. "All right," I said, "when you get a man's job, call me!" She never called. So, I went out on my own. Walked into this firm and worked my way up, while attending night school for my MBA, and in less than ten years, compare that to any office boy—

I'm explaining myself—as if I have to justify. I have nothing to feel guilty about. All my life I played by the rules, even when I didn't know what they were! OK. OK. I made a mistake. I stupidly let the office bleed into my personal life, like the ding-dong receptionist.

When he found out we were working together, he threw a fit; tried to get assigned a different job; told me I could take care of the typing. It was obvious the moron couldn't write that proposal without me, but then, when it was finished, and he asked me out for a drink, I was flattered. I wrote three-quarters of that proposal myself, and I didn't feel triumphant until he asked me, tail between his legs, out for a drink!

Of course, he couldn't hold his liquor. Of course, he drank too much. Of course, he started in right away with the touchie feelies. I told him politely, I wasn't interested. "Bitch!" "That's right," I said, paid half the tab and got up to leave. "Bimbo!" "No!" I threw my drink in his face and walked out.

I should have anticipated: the rude comments; the disgusting noises passing the xerox; the rumors going round via stockboys and secretaries: I was a nymphomaniac, into whips, chains, old men, women, children—cats. I got obscene phone calls, so I bought a rape whistle. He followed me home at night, I took cabs. But, when I received what I assumed were a copy of his sex organs, greatly enlarged, in my in-box, I confronted him. And he accused me of being a virgin. To my face he said that! (*Beat*) All this time I still didn't think he was a threat; until the nasty, stinking, filthy rumors reached this floor.

Maybe it was in my head, but now it was too late. I kept quiet for so long, anything I said now in my defense would only make me look guilty! Or paranoid. Well, of course, I'm paranoid. I'm a woman. When I have to justify even not sleeping with that pig. Who knows what insignificant trivial detail he'd dug up and blown all out of proportion. I had no idea what I was defending myself against. (*Beat*) And the worst of it was, it wasn't me, in all his perversion, he was interested in, anyway.

Today . . . I was passed up for partnership. (*Half beat*) I walked straight into his office, ten minutes ago, I said, "OK, what is it? Is it just a fuck you want? Let's go pal, right here on your desk! Pull out the original and we'll measure it up to the copy!"

And that's when he did it. He used that word. I wasn't prepared for it. He shot it right at me. While leaning so smugly over his desk. Leering at me. Drooling. Spit it right into my face: "You stupid cunt."

(*Calmly*) And I picked up the marble paperweight sitting on his desk and bashed his stupid head in.

Ashes, Ashes

TAMMY RYAN

She used to say my parents were the crazy ones. If you ask me, they're just borin'. But sometimes you need borin'. I mean, like, life is like this constant war goin' on outside your head; you need some kinda relief from it now and then.

Like at school. This kills me. They're always tellin' you to speak out for your rights, like they did in the sixties, right, thirty years ago. So one day in social studies, I start speaking out for my rights. I tole Mr. Katz, I thought everybody in the world was crazy. Teachers, parents, politicians, cops, cabdrivers, housewives, people on TV—everybody! Walkin' around, talkin', acting like everything is all right. When it's obvious everything is not all right.

I'm on a roll, all right, going on about how nobody's gonna be happy till we blow ourselves up. Telling me to prepare for my future, when my future looks like a nuclear bomb, ok? It tastes like ashes! Katz got his back to me, erasing the board, like I'm not even here. Nobody says a word. Just Julie clappin' in the background. When Katz whips around and throws his eraser at me. A cloud of chalk explodes on my chest. Then he sent me to the Nurse.

What he doesn't understand is that for me and Julie, the bomb is not like something you discuss in social studies. It's something we've lived with. Ever since we were little, we waited for it to drop. We waited for it like the sun comin' up tomorrow. Like Christmas always came. Like our wedding days someday. When we were little kids, we played this game: walking down the street, one of us would look at the other and say: "Do you think it's gonna be now? Are you ready for it?" We'd convince ourselves it'd be the next black second:

BAM. Mushroom Cloud. The end. I know, I know, the cold war is over. All right, so maybe it's not gonna be one big bomb. Maybe it's gonna be a slow leak.

Like Chernobyl. Yeah. Anybody remember that? Me and Jul spent two weeks watchin' the sky, waiting for that radioactive cloud and everybody else acted like: So what? It's no big deal: go to school, go to work, go shopping. I opened my mouth to ask a question about the level of radioactivity in the milk and my father goes crazy, screamin' at me: NOT AT THE KITCHEN TABLE! Like I brought up Hiroshima. I didn't want to drink the milk if it was radioactive.

Ok, maybe me and Jul did read *On the Beach* and we were waiting for everybody to start throwing up and nobody did. But wasn't anybody else scared? Julie's father was the only person we knew who reacted. He bought canned food and powdered milk and we all camped out in his basement. He told us the government had a plan to hold nuclear weapons over people's heads till we all turned into a bunch of sheep. "But what happens when the bombs blow up?" we asked him. "All the sheep die." That's what he said. Sick.

When me and Jul were in kindergarten they made us play "ring around the rosie," you know, all the kids laughing and singing, "Ring around the rosie, pockets full of posie . . . " When we got to the part, "Ashes, ashes, all fall down," me and Jul stopped laughin'. What was so funny about being burnt to ashes? Later I found out this harmless little nursery rhyme is really about the black plague. Ashes, ashes, we all fall down. All the sheep die. I guess the human race still got the same sense of humor. And I still don't get the joke.

Blind

ELISABETH SAMPSON

WOMAN: Grey was the first color I ever saw. (*She breathes.*)
Then there was red. (*She exhales.*)
I can't begin to tell you how grateful I am. Yet it's all so
confusing. A whirlwind of confusion. Realize, of course, I've
never seen a whirlwind before, but I'm going to. I'm going to
see everything. (*She turns.*)
I want to have the charges on the boy dropped. Yes, I do
understand that I am walking around with a concussion, but
that doesn't give you any right not to listen to me. I belong to
a family of taxpayers. I have a right to be treated like your
boss, not some crazy woman that got jumped at the Seven-
Eleven two weeks ago. (*She rubs her head.*)
Grey was the first color I ever saw. But it wasn't until I saw
red that I knew what grey meant to me. I needed that next
color, my own blood on the greyed pavement, to know that I
hadn't been looking at merely nothing. Nothingness has a color.
Mr. Bowman, my whole life doctors have been telling my
family and myself that my blindness was a fixable condition.
It was some sort of faulty connection in a nerve. For twenty-
six years they've been sending us bills for pumping me full of
drugs and for cutting me open to take a look. They've
charged my family tens of thousands of dollars, and given us
nothing but their confusion that I was still blind. In one
night, that kid solved my problem, yet all he got was the
seven dollars in my wallet. Do you honestly think that a person like that kid just whams blind ladies in the head for a
hobby? He gave me a miracle, and I'm refusing to press
charges. Yet you keep holding him, calling him a public
threat. I am a taxpayer, and I refuse to let you use my tax
money to hold that child. (*Pause*)

It's obvious that you don't care, you're just some monkey in a double-breasted uniform. You use that soft voice, yeah, I can read insincerity in my earshot, and I tell you, I have good ears. I've spent twenty-six years looking at you with these ears. Twenty-six years of excuse-me's and I'm sorry and being sent down the wrong street because I couldn't read the sign. Please, I'm trying to make a point here. That kid gave me something that twenty-six years of doctors and drugs and operations couldn't. But you keep bringing up laws and society and crime. Which crime?

Maybe, on (*Date two weeks ago*), I was only trying to get a pack of cigarettes—you look surprised. Didn't you know that blind women can smoke too? I prefer Camels light, and I can tell just as well as anyone when I'm given the wrong brand. Maybe I was only trying to buy some smokes, but I got a miracle. And yeah, it hurt, so did all the operations I've had. You think brain surgery is a day at the fair?

Hey. I made an appointment to talk to you and you're treating me like someone who doesn't have a right to voice an opinion in this situation. Mr. Bowman, I was the victim. I lost a pint of blood, but I'll give it back. You need to believe me that I will fight for that boy's defense. What kind of society raises thirteen-year-old boys to attack blind women? The same society that kept turning me down for employment. I know what world he's been in. A world that keeps everybody but the perfect out.

Bright Girls, Stupid Lives

JUDY SHEEHAN

(Allison addresses the audience. She is so sad, she can barely speak. She is wearing an old sweatsuit and appears disheveled.)

ALLISON: Never ever think that you're too good for someone or something. 'Cause then you'll lose them. You won't be paying attention and it'll all slip away.

I don't know who I am today. I'm a social security number that's going to apply for unemployment. I'm a non-writer, non-woman who has lost everything she didn't value in the first place. I stopped crying a long time ago.

If I get the chance, I won't make that mistake again. I won't think I'm too good for the work or the guy or whatever. Right now, I can't imagine what I'm good enough for. How could I have been so stupid?

My friends all talk like fortune cookies but I can't really hear them. They think I'm ignoring them, but the truth is, every time they say something to cheer me up, I just can't hear it. It's like static. I should see a doctor.

I could become a bank teller in three weeks. Don't look at me like that. I'm entitled. Ever been fired from a demeaning job by your not-too-bright lover who is also dumping you? It's not one of life's peak experiences, let me tell you. So until you have survived it, I suggest you save your judgmental pity for the next Republican convention.

Antlers on the Wall

AMY SILBERMAN

Driving from Boston to Andover, you spoke of coon hunting. In Salem, you mentioned your skeet shooting. From your breast pocket, you pulled out a picture of a twenty-pound bluefish you caught off the coast of Jamaica last week. What pride shone in those grey-blue eyes! How long will the photograph decorate that pocket? Your children: bluefish, raccoon, and skeet.

Leaving Massachusetts, you recalled deer hunting in Iowa; mounting a buck's antlers, dismembering a doe, the tenuousness of the task, how exhausting it had been. I couldn't tell you then. No matter how much I liked New Hampshire, I couldn't tell you then that there was life in my body when there was death in your pocket. Where there were antlers on the wall. Driving along the coast, the pictures in my head were of bludgeoned seals, of maimed babies. If my news was that I shot a boar and the carcass awaited you in my apartment, you'd be thrilled. If I were a fifty-foot schooner with a cargo of swordfish, you'd be in ecstasy.

I wanted to strangle your fishing rod. Swallow your rifle. Castrate your magnum. And, for a brief moment near Nashua, give birth to a bear-skin rug.

Equal Unto the Angels

STEPHANIE SIMPSON

(Belva, bruised and bandaged, waits at a bus stop. She is a beauty operator.)

BELVA: Now the fact is that I'm glad I ran away, but I'm just as scared as I can be. I'm scared he's gonna find me and beat me to death. I'm really scared he's gonna find me and ask me to forgive him and take him back. I know how he'll put his hand real sad-like on my face, and I'll just set there feelin' those sweaty, shaky fingers on my cheek and knowin' that he is hurtin', but also knowin' that he'd do it again. That's the crazy part. I mean, he'll prob'ly even start cryin' and sweet-talkin', and I'll just be settin' there, starin' at the floor, tryin' to figure out *how* to forgive him. That's what gets me worried. I can't quite see my way clear to it. I mean, I wanna forgive him, but I also wanna get away from him. And he's not going to understand that. 'Cause I think, to him, when I say I forgive him, that means I'm takin' him back. It means I'm sayin' to him, "It's all right. I'm long-sufferin' enough that you can beat me and beat me and I can take it til you stop or I die, whichever comes first." He kinda gets my forgiveness mixed up with my permission. But that's not how I mean it. I think I wanna be able to forgive him the way Jesus forgave Mary Magdalene. He just said, "Go and sin no more." He just set her free. That's how I wanna forgive Fred. I wanna do it so I can just set us free, me and him both.

Last night I had this nightmare that the Rapture came, and I was standin' up before the Lord bein' judged, and I asked God for Tahiti, and He said, "Yes," but then Fred appeared, lookin' real mad—he'd found me in the middle of the Rapture. And I said, "Oh Lord, do I have to take him with me?" And the Lord said, "Well, I'm sorry, but you married him and you're joined together for all eternity." And I woke up in a panic, thinkin', I'll never get away and Fred'll never change. So right away, I went to the Bible, to see if there was a chance my nightmare could come true. So I turned to the New Testament, and right there, in the twentieth chapter of Luke, Verses 34–36, I found this:

"And Jesus answering said unto them, The children of this world marry and are given in marriage:

but they which shall be accounted worthy to obtain that world, and the resurrection of the dead, neither marry, nor are given in marriage:

Neither can they die anymore; for they are equal unto the angels."

And that was just the greatest comfort to me. 'Cause that's exactly what I want to be: equal unto the angels, free and equal.

Another Paradise

DONNA SPECTOR

(Birdie Mae is remembering her family, including her husband, Hiram, and her daughter, Neva.)

BIRDIE MAE: I bin settin' here thinkin' 'bout how all a them kids leaned on me, thinkin' I was strong. An' Hiram too, he leaned on me, an' I didn't never *feel* real strong. But there's somethin' 'bout bein' a mother, don't matter how ol' you are, people jes' wanna crawl right onto yer lap an' have you hold 'em. An' don't matter if you never boiled a egg, soon as yer a mother, you gotta make biscuits an' fried chicken an' pie.

When my first chile come, I'd never in all a my fifteen years swung a chicken round an' round till its neck was broke. I'd watched my mama do it, so I knew what to do. I took holt a that chicken an' started in swingin'. I swung an' swung till my arm near to fell off at the shoulder, an' that neck wouldn't break. All a them chickens started in to squawkin' like they was tryin' to bring the night on early. Well, I felt such a fool, an' my arm was bleedin' from mad chicken scratches. But it was me er the chicken jes' then, so I run on over to a big ol' tree an' started in smashin' that chicken into the trunk till I broke ever' bone in its body. Now Neva, the baby, was yellin' so hard she started in chokin'. I threw that bloody chicken against the side a the house an' went runnin' to pick up my baby. I got blood all over 'er, of course. What a mess! The sun was near settin', so I knew Hiram'd be home. I quick washed off Neva an' the battered ol' chicken, stoked up the fire, an' threw the chicken in the oven. When Hiram come home, he said he smelt somethin' funny, an' sure enough, I'd cooked that damn ol' chicken with all its feathers on. (*Sighs*)

Well, it's jes' like Hiram said, the Lord don't care fer pretense. When you do somethin' wrong, ain't no way to hide it.

Shelter

CARIDAD SVICH

(Eileen is standing, looking at herself in a mirror, naked. She is a sensual woman in her mid-thirties; an innocent spirit, weary but relentless, lucid in the face of catastrophe. Her brother, Stevie, is seated near her, reading the newspaper.)

EILEEN: You've always been ashamed of me. Ashamed of having a sister. Men. Men always want brothers. Sisters are an embarrassment. You gotta keep them covered up.

I want to look at myself.

How am I supposed to do that if I don't take off my clothes? I haven't looked at my body in years. I get up, throw something over my head and. . . . Oh. My heart. I'd forgotten it beat. Funny how you can forget you're alive in the world. . . . And this space between my breasts. . . . It's so . . . tender. (*Pause*)

Men don't like bodies. They like parts: legs, thigh, breast. They'd take 'em home if they could, leave what they don't want somewhere else.

Sometimes I dream my body parts are strewn all over the yard hiding among what's left of our garden.

And you're standing there, planting them inside the earth so they can't grow, so they're buried forever among the roots and the slugs, broken up and tangled in the soil till they have no memory of ever having been parts that belonged to a body, that were something whole.

You'd think my body was a crime.

You know how long it's been since I've even looked at my belly button?

I want to stick my tongue in it.

Just to feel what it tastes like.

Desdemona

PAULA VOGEL

(Emilia, Desdemona's nurse and caretaker, talks with her about love, sex, and her marriage to Iago. They are sitting and drinking in the kitchen where Emilia works.)

EMILIA: When I was married in the Church, the knot tied beneath the Virgin's nose, my head was filled with all sorts of girl-nonsense. I looked forward to the bed with as much joy as any girl after a hard day. And my strength! I could be tackling the wash from dawn to dusk and still have sweat enough left over for any man. And then Iago—well, he was still a lad, with the softness of a boy, and who could tell he'd turn into the man? (*Emilia pauses to drink.*)

But all that nonsense was knocked out of me by the nights. Night following night, as sure as the day's work came after. I'd stretch myself out on the bed, you see, waiting for my good man to come to me and be my mate—as the priest said he could—but then—but then I saw it didn't matter what had gone on between us—the fights, my crying, a good meal or a cold one. Days could pass without a word between us—and he'd take his fill of me the same. No matter, it was the same. I could have been the bed itself. And so, you see, I vowed not to be there for him. As he'd be lying on me in the dark, I'd picture up my rosary, so real I could kiss the silver. And I'd start at the blessed cross itself, while he was somewhere doing his business above, and I'd say the first wooden bead, and then I'd finger the next bead in my mind, and then onto the next—(*Stops*) But I never did make it to the medallion. He'd be all through with me by the time of the third "Hail Mary." (*Pause*)

Does my lady know what I'm saying? Ah, well, men are making fools of themselves over you. The Ambassador is traipsing from the mainland just to hold onto your skirt; and your husband—(*Emilia stops herself.*)—Well, maybe it's all different for the likes of you.

And then, maybe not. It's hard to be seeing, when you're young and men watch you when you pass them by, and the talking stops between them. But all in all, in time you'll know. Women just don't figure in their heads—not the one who hangs the wash, not Bianca—and not even you, m'lady. (*Brighter*) And that's why I'm ready to leave the whole pack of them behind and go with you and the Ambassador. Oh, to see my husband's face tomorrow morning! When he finds out that I can get along by myself, with no thanks to his plotting and hatching: to have a nest egg of my own under my rump! —but it's leave him now or be counting my beads through the years, waiting for his last breath.

The Fish Story

NAOMI WALLACE

(A young woman is telling a story. She has a lure box with her.)

It was almost like they knew they were going to be crucified. First they would lie still on your palm, as though dead. Only a slight tremor, at one end or the other, gave their trick away. It was this moment. This moment of calm right before it happened, that I liked most, when their tender, fleshy bodies, studded with black dirt, would lay in my hand like the trust of an old friend. At seven years old, that glistening body of plumped worminess was more beautiful to me than any. . . . (*Breaks off.*)

But when the hook came up close, the thing would start to writhe like all hell-fire was upon it. *(Beat)* It isn't true that worms wriggle when they're threaded on the hook. Those who say they do never hooked a worm in their life. No, worms don't wriggle, they writhe.

It didn't bother my father. He'd just pluck the worm from the jar and thread it on the hook without blinking an eye. When he wasn't looking, I'd whisper "hush, hush" to the worm and when it turned its stomach to me, that pink band that circles its body like a wedding ring, I'd strike fast, straight through the center. (*She opens the box and carefully lays out some lures.*)

No one made me do it but myself and for while I felt sorry for the worms, I loved hauling in the bass. And me and my father would stand side by side, casting the deep stream pools. We'd bet on who would holler first "I got one!"

Daddy was my friend. He liked fishing the way I liked it. When he cast a good one, his lips would go white and his chin would tremble just a little as he waited for a strike. Sometimes one of his ears would go red with all that waiting. Not both of them, just the left one. Red as a worm. (*Singing*) Oh my love is like a red, red worm. Once I hooked that red ear. I was fly fishing and I hauled back to snap the line and toss it on a new patch of water and (*Beat. She screams as though she were her father.*) That's how he sounded. (*She polishes some lures.*)

I didn't know at first what had happened so I kept jerking at the rod until my Daddy caught hold of my line with his free hand and jerked back; the rod flew out of my hands and snapped in two on the ground between us. And there hung my fly with three hooks, one hook embedded in that red ear which was redder than I'd ever seen it. He made me get it out. He didn't say a word, just opened his lure box, took out a pair of pliers and handed them to me. (*Beat*) When a bluegill swallows an artificial fly or a spinner, it usually hooks down into its lungs. You see, bluegills have small mouths and what goes in doesn't come out. If it isn't your favorite lure, you can cut the line and throw the fish back in. They say the creek water will rust a hook out of a fish's mouth in forty-eight hours. If it's your favorite lure, and one time it was my favorite, you just have to pull. That's when a piece of the lung will come out with the hook. (*Beat*) But an ear isn't a fish. And yet my father's ear was tougher than a catfish lip. I had to twist and pull. Twist and pull. The ear fought me. It wouldn't let go. It held on tight. My father just sat there and I knew if I didn't get it out, if he had to do it himself, then . . . well, twist and pull. Twist and pull. Finally it tore. The ear. And out the hook came.

He let me choose. My father was good about that. He said I could have a spanking, without my shorts on, or eat a worm as my punishment for not looking behind me when I'd swung the rod. So I dug down into the jar and pulled one out, praying I'd grab a dead one. But that worm must have been sleeping 'cause the moment it got near my mouth it

LIVERPOOL JOHN MOORES UNIVERSITY
LEARNING SERVICES

sparked like a firecracker trying to get loose. (*Beat*) Well, I looked at the worm and if a worm can look, it did so at me. I'd never had one before, though once my Daddy let me choose between biting the tail off a grasshopper or not watching television for two whole weeks when I spilled a can of paint in the garage. I went for the grasshopper. Like a saltine cracker, almost exactly, when I ate it. (*She hangs the lures on her outstretched arm as she speaks until they hang like decorations in a row.*)

They say a worm has seven hearts and that if you cut it in the right places, two or three of the pieces will live. The problem was, I didn't know where the hearts were or where to bite. I held it up to the light but I couldn't see anything but red worm. I put it halfway into my mouth. I figured biting it halfway was a choice. Random would kill it for sure. I closed my eyes but I couldn't bite down. The half of the worm that was inside started tickling the roof of my mouth like how the dentist does. I started to laugh but then Daddy started shouting for me to do it. He was saying "Now, now, now." (*Beat.*)

Then Daddy slapped me on the back of the head and I bit down.

I only use artificials now. I like the sound of their names: Switchback, Rapala, Zarco spinner, Bass magnet, Zephyr Puppy, Double-headed jig, and Jitterbug. Twelve-pound line. Eight-pound line. Six-pound line. I was using four-pound line later that day. I cast my line right between a fallen tree and rock ledge. It fell on the water with hardly a splash. I twitched the line once. Twice. Just before the third twitch and reel, the bass struck it.

There must have been some magic to the flesh of that worm I ate because that afternoon I landed a four-pound small-mouthed bass. Almost snapped my line. It took me fifteen minutes to bring that monster close enough to the bank so my father could scoop it up in the net. Daddy and I skinned it right there and cooked it over the fire. I can tell you I was proud that day. And Daddy was proud of me too. He kissed me on the mouth four times, one kiss for each pound of that bass. Have you ever made your father that proud of you? I mean, that proud? Four times. He kissed me four times. On the mouth. Have you ever? Four times? On the mouth? (*Beat*) I can show you. It's hard to tell you just how it went unless I show you. That's how proud he was. That's how. Yes. And I closed my eyes because I had to. Because if a worm has seven hearts it could have eight and I wanted him to know I could take it. And I took it. On the mouth. But once it's cut. The worm. You never can tell just which parts have been killed and which parts will crawl away and start over because all of the parts are moving. All of the parts are trying to live. But only one or two of them do. Live.

I'll tell you a secret: I'm not very a good daughter. It was worse. His pride in me. Worse. Than eating that worm. Silly, isn't it? Know what I mean? Do you? Four times. On the mouth. That's how it started. Then we went home to tell Mother about my bass.

You wouldn't know it, would you? To look at me. Some of this, here (*Motions to parts of her body, slowly.*) isn't really alive anymore. Deceptive, isn't it? How can one look at the body and see nothing but the whole of it. But I know. I know which parts went on and lived and which parts gave up and died. I can tell them apart just by touching them. (*She gently touches herself in different places, not necessarily sexual parts of her body.*) Can you tell them apart? If you touch yourself, here and here, or there and there? Go on. Try it. That's it. Can you tell just which parts of you are dead and which parts of you are still alive? (*Beat*) Got it? All right then. When you're ready. (*Beat*) Let's go fishing.

Momma's Little Helper

ROSE WEAVER

Momma please don't cry. Please. He gone now. For a little while anyway. Come on. Let's sing our favorite song, okay. I'll start it this time. "Don't sit under the apple tree with anyone else but me, anyone else but. . . . " Please don't cry. You know what? I got an "A" on my English test Friday. And Mr. Becker accepted me in the Upward Bound Program. He even promised me a job. So after I have the baby I can pay Grandma to watch it while I keep going to school. And he said, "Rosetta, if you keep making grades like that, why, you can go to college." I know you'd like that, wouldn't you Momma.

Oh, before I forget, I got a letter from Michael today. He's in Germany now. He says the Army's not going to send him to Vietnam. I don't care one way or the other. He didn't want to marry me before he left and I can do without him now. Momma. . . . How come you let Daddy beat on you every weekend? We ain't done nothing to him. You cook him ham and biscuits like he likes 'em and make him a nice lunch every morning. You have his favorite supper ready every night. I wash and iron his khakis. Johnny cleans his shoes. Bobby washes his truck. Marci runs his bath. When he decides to bathe. Leroy gets his Luckies. But every Friday night he gets mad for no reason. Oh, God, Momma! I . . . I've got a surprise for you. I know how you like surprises. Remember two years ago when I first started my baby-sitting jobs? Well, I've been saving a little here and there. This is a money order made out to you for two hundred dollars. It's the down payment for a house. Your house, Momma. We can move out of this . . . place. Oh, you're so pretty when you smile. I love it when you're smiling and singing. You know what else, Momma? When I grow up and become a big movie star, I'm gone get you anything you want.

Chips on My Shoulder

ROSE WEAVER

I don't have chips on my shoulders.
Uh uh.
I knocked 'em off a long time ago.
When I realized that cussing y'all Jews and Gentiles out,
And calling y'all every kinda fucker I could think of,
Just narrowed y'all's minds even more about my potential,
I adapted myself.

It didn't help me to blame y'all every minute of my day
For what y'all's dead relatives did to my dead people.
Theys all dead and nobody can tell me that we know how
    they felt.

I sho can't imagine what it felt like
To have shackles on my feet
And chains around my neck
And crammed like a sardine
On the bottom of a ship
Crossing the ocean with nothing to eat.

You don't know what it felt like
To burn at a stake
In a smoky flame
'Cause some fanatical lady down the road said
You was a witch.

And he can't know
The feeling of baking in an oven.

Shit!

Any a y'all got chips on your shoulders?

I don't. Uh uh.
I knocked mine off a looooonnng time ago.

Joan

MARJORIE ZOHN

(Joan is very pregnant.)

JOAN: This, what you see here, is not planned parenthood. It's ruptured condom. Take a good look at the failure of modern technology: human life. But let me give you a little background on my situation. *(Removes pregnancy pillow and puts it underneath head.)* So he's on top, I'm down here, we're going at it, and he says—wow, this feels really good. Really really good. And I'm thinking, hey, this can only mean one thing. This can only mean that two percent of surgical rubber that your mother warned you about. So I'm saying, hey honey, hello, yoo hoo, do you think we can have a timeout here to check . . . but as soon as I say timeout, I know I'm done for. He's a sports freak. And the thought process goes—timeout, basketball, women's basketball, women, Christie Brinkley and BLAM BANG WHOOPEE HIP HOORAY HALLELUJAH oh my god oh my god oh my god was it good for you? And me—thinking really hard, multiplying the number of days past ovulation times the number of sperm racing to violate my unwilling egg times my special percentage of shit luck— me, I say, "Yes, daddy." And he freaks. And I freak. And then we go get pasta. *(She replaces pregnancy pillow.)*

Eight months later, I eat chocolate chips with my pasta. He eats at his old girlfriend's, so I don't know what she serves him. The same old story, you've heard it a million times. But wait—why didn't I get an abortion? Why didn't I hit the delete key, press the eject button, white it out, purge it up, record over it, return it for a store credit, dump it into the water supply and forget about it? *(Beat)* I don't know, I think I just didn't have the money at the time.

Biographies

NANCY BAGSHAW-REASONER was born in Pennsylvania, but, having spent the last eighteen years in Minnesota, she claims native status in the Land of the Vikings. For twenty years, she trod the boards successfully as an actress, only to discover that her passion was for the writers. So she became one. Her plays include *Nancy with the Laughing Face, After the Ball, The Pilgrimage,* and *Tough Love.* Her newest effort is an entertainment concerning Jack the Ripper, called *Noblesse Oblige.* Nancy lives with her husband, Fred Reasoner, their children, and a couple of animals.

DEBORAH BALEY has been a company member at Perseverance Theatre in Juneau, Alaska since 1980. Her first play, *The Last Frontier Club,* won the Alaska Repertory Theatre's DramaQuest competition in 1987. Her other plays include *Signs of Life* (produced at Perseverance under a Rockefeller Foundation Playwriting Fellowship), *Blue Moon Over Graceland* (a Noh Drama about Elvis Presley), and *Into the Fire* (to be produced at Rites and Reason Theatre in Providence, RI, in 1994). Ms. Baley is one of ten artists chosen by the National Endowment for the Arts to participate in a two-month residency in Mexico in 1994.

SALLIE BINGHAM is a novelist, essayist, and playwright, whose works include four novels (*After Such Knowledge, The Touching Hand, Small Victories,* and *Upstate*), her autobiographical memoir *Passion and Prejudice,* numerous short stories, and seven produced plays (*Milk of Paradise, The Wall Between, Couvade, Paducah, In the Presence, Hopscotch,* and *The Awakening*). Her plays have been produced by The

Women's Project, Actors Theatre of Louisville, Horse Cave Theatre, Mill Mountain Theatre, and several universities. *In the Presence,* from which the monologue in this volume is taken, won the Mill Mountain Theatre New Play Award for 1993. Through her work with the Kentucky Foundation for Women, she has been a major supporter of women artists and has helped to bring about social change through the arts.

ELSIE ERVIN BOCK was born and raised in the Mississippi Delta. She did her undergraduate work at Delta State College in Cleveland, MS, and her graduate work at Duke. For the past twenty years, she has been teaching at Lynchburg College, where she is Professor of English. Ms. Bock has had several stories published in literary magazines *(Crosscurrents, Wind, Virginia,* and *Oasis)*, and in 1993, one of her essays appeared in *The Washington Post.* She has also written one full-length and several one-act plays—and she has just completed her first novel.

BETH BROWDE has had a varied career in the arts. As a classical guitarist, she earned a Master of Music degree at Yale and toured throughout the United States and Europe. As a singer, she spent a season with the Light Opera of Manhattan, appeared at the Kool Jazz Festival, did some studio work, and toured the New York Public Schools with a group called Vocal Jazz. As an actress, she worked primarily with new playwrights, Mac Wellman, Sonia Taitz, Dan Brederman, and Neena Beeber. She wrote and appeared in two one-woman plays, *Lapse in the Main Stream* and *Temporary Shelter,* for the National Theatre in Washington, DC. She is currently working on a novel, *All or Nothing,* and working toward an MFA in fiction at Columbia University School of the Arts.

HEIDI CARLA was born and raised in Providence, RI. She attended graduate programs at Brandeis and Brown Universities. Her plays have been produced at the Trinity

Repertory Company Conservatory, Company One in Hartford, CT, and Brown University. Her play *Vesta Tilley in America* won the 1993 Mary Roberts Rinehart Award for best play. Ms. Carla has held writing fellowships from the Edward F. Albee Foundation and Hedgebrook Residencies.

BRIDGET CARPENTER's plays, which have been produced in Australia and Scotland as well as in the United States, include *Divine Providence, An Evening with Tiny, The Dog Who Was a Performance Artist,* and *The Ride.* She has received grants from the Brown University Magaziner Fund, the Ford Foundation, and the National Endowment for the Arts. While living in Los Angeles, she was an Associate Mentor Playwright at the Mark Taper Forum. She dedicates *The Ride* to Marguerite MacDonald, Molly, Taffy, and Madison.

PEARL CLEAGE is an Atlanta-based writer whose plays include *Flyin' West, Hotspice, Puppetplay,* and *Late Bus to Mecca* (published in Heinemann's *Playwriting Women). Flyin' West* was commissioned and premiered by the Alliance Theatre and was the recipient of an AT&T OnStage Award. Ms. Cleage is also the author of a book of essays, *Deals with the Devil and Other Reasons to Riot.* She is currently playwright-in-residence at Spelman College.

ALICE EVE COHEN is a playwright, solo theatre artist, and composer. Her works have been presented on four continents, at venues including New York Theatre Workshop, The Public Theatre, The Women's Project, Manhattan Punch Line, La Mama, Theatre for the New City, the Smithsonian Institute, New Orleans Museum of Art, and international theatre festivals. Her plays include *Oklahoma Samovar, The Play That Knows What You Want, Without Heroes,* and *Goliath on 74th Street vs. the Woman Who Loved Vegetables.* Her awards include a New York State Council on the Arts

Playwriting Fellowship, National Endowment for the Arts production grants, ASCAP awards for music-theatre, and Meet the Composer awards.

KAREN CRONACHER's plays question the conventional representation of women and translate the results of current theoretical and historical scholarship into entertaining satire. Her plays include *Unspeakable Pleasures, Traindreams, Scavengers,* and *Unsafe Secretions and Panic Situations.* Ms. Cronacher's work has won awards in the Young Playwright's Festival, the American College Theatre Festival, and the Clauder Competition. She has won the Forbes-Heermans Playwriting Prize and the student competition of the Jane Chambers Playwriting Award. Ms. Cronacher is also a published feminist scholar with a Ph.D. from the University of Washington.

EDWIDGE DANTICAT was born in Port-au-Prince, Haiti. Her work has been published in *The Caribbean Writer, Short Fictions by Women, The Providence Journal,* and other publications. Her first play, *The Creation of Adam,* was produced by Rites and Reason Theatre in Providence, RI. Her second play, *Dreams Like Me,* was produced at Brown University in 1993. Edwidge is an emerging playwright who also works in other genres, including poetry and screenwriting. She is currently finishing her first novel.

EVE ENSLER's works include *The Depot* (directed by Joanne Woodward and starring Shirley Knight), *Ladies, Scooncat, Chamomile Tea, Cinderella/Cendrillon* (with Anne Bogart), *Coming from Nothing,* and *Reef and Particle.* Her plays have been produced at the Music Theatre Group, HOME for Contemporary Theatre and Art, L.A.T.C., The Westwood Playhouse, The Samuel Beckett Theatre, Interart Theatre, The Actor's Studio, and The Women's Project. As a screenwriter, Ms. Ensler has completed *The Queen* and *Sissy Wonder and The Ball Tree.* She is currently writing a feature film for

Paramount. She is a founding member of Anonymous Women for Peace and Women Helping Women.

KATHLEEN GERMANN is an actress who lives in the Hudson Valley. She has an interest in plays that address issues relevant to women. This is her first published work.

JOLENE GOLDENTHAL's play, *The Other Sonya*, was a finalist for the O'Neill Theatre Conference. Her plays for women, *Remembering Rachel* and *Mequasset by the Sea* were, respectively, finalist and semi-finalist for the Berman Award. Ms. Goldenthal is presently completing her new play, *How We Met and Other Events*.

JANE HILL is one of the co-founders of Dell'Arte, Inc. and currently serves as Development Director for the Dell'Arte Players Company and the Dell'Arte School of Physical Theatre. She has a wide range of directing, teaching, writing, consulting, and performing credits. She created *Nothing Remarkable* from the abandoned letters and family records of a Eureka, CA, farm woman, and *Nothing Less Than Love*, a musical, grew out of interviews with thirty daughters and mothers. Ms. Hill's most recent venture is a one-person show, *Getting It*, a darkly humorous view of four women in mid-life and beyond, from which "Margaret's Workout" and "Still Blooming" are excerpted.

TINA HOWE is the author of *The Nest*, *Birth and After Birth*, *Museum*, *The Art of Dining*, *Painting Churches*, *Coastal Disturbances*, *Approaching Zanzibar*, and *One Shoe Off*. These works premiered at the Los Angeles Actors Theatre, the New York Shakespeare Festival, the Kennedy Center, and the Second Stage. Her awards include an Obie for Distinguished Playwriting, 1983; an Outer Critics Circle Award, 1983; a Rockefeller grant, 1984; an NEA Fellowship, 1985; a Guggenheim Fellowship, 1990; and an American Academy of Arts and Letters Award in Literature, 1993. In 1987, she received a Tony nomination for Best Play, and in 1988 she received an honorary degree from Bowdoin College. Ms. Howe currently teaches playwriting at Hunter College and NYU. She is a council member of the Dramatists Guild.

SAMANTHA GRACE KELLY received a B.A. in English Literature from Smith College. Recently a writer-in-residence with the Roger Hendricks Simon Studio in New York, she previously studied acting and knows how difficult it can be to find good monologues for women. "Little Girl Dreams" and "Loreli" are excerpted from her play, *Remote Control*, which was performed at the La Mama La Galleria and the Cornelia Street Cafe Theatre. Other plays include *Dr. Watson* and *Intimate Strangers*, which was performed at an Ensemble Studio Theatre Festival. She received a Poets and Writers grant and is a member of the Dramatists Guild.

SHERRY KRAMER's plays have been produced in New York at the Second Stage Theatre, the Soho Rep, and the Ensemble Studio Theatre as well as at Yale Rep, the Woolly Mammoth Theatre, and many other theatres here and abroad. She has received playwriting fellowships from the NEA and the New York Foundation for the Arts. Her plays include *What a Man Weighs* (Weissberger Playwriting Award, New York Drama League Award, and the Marvin Taylor New Play Award), *The Wall of Water* (the L.A. Women in Theatre New Play Award), *David's RedHaired Death* (the Jane Chambers Playwriting Award), *Things That Break, Women Are Work, Partial Objects*, and a music-theatre adaptation of Bulgakov's *The Master and Margarita*.

SARAH JANE LAPP explores theatre's role in community education, religion, and women's healthcare. Born in Minneapolis, and enriched by COMPASS's wonderful mentor-writers, she divides her time between the visual and literary arts at education and local community arts centers including the Walker

Art Center, COMPASS, and Mixed Blood Theatre Company. She is currently enrolled in Brown University's undergraduate Creative Writing Program.

JOAN LIPKIN is the Artistic Director of that Uppity Theatre Company in St. Louis, where she founded the Alternate Currents/Direct Currents Series and After Rodney, a poetry performance group of white women and women of color. Her plays include *Some of My Best Friends Are . . .*, *He's Having Her Baby* (co-written with Tom Clear), *Love and Work and Other Four-Letter Words*, *Small Domestic Acts*, *One Sunday Morning*, and *The Pornography Letters*, among others. Her work is included in *Upstaging Big Daddy*, *Contemporary Feminist Theatres*, and the forthcoming *Feminists, Theatres, Social Change*, and *Fallow Fields*. She is a member of the Dramatists Guild.

FLORENCIA LOZANO grew up in Newton, Massachusetts, but her parents are originally from Argentina. She attended Cornell and then Brown, where she received her B.A. Florencia is an actress and playwright currently living in New York City, where she is a member of the graduate acting program at NYU's Tisch School. She dedicates *Under Her Breath* to her niece, Julia Margarita Drachman.

MICHEL MAGEE is a writer and artist whose articles, interviews, short stories, and editorial cartoons have been featured in many venues, including *Ms. Magazine*, *Travel & Leisure*, *Yankee Magazine*, *Manhattan Comic News*, and *Cape Cod Life*. Her work has been presented in live theatre, and on radio and television. An artist with national and international honors to her credit, Ms. Magee's paintings have been exhibited in New York and Paris. She is the founder and artistic director of the Nantucket Readers Theatre, a showcase for works in progress. She lives on Nantucket and recently completed a screenplay for PBS. She is currently working on her second play.

MADELEINE MARTIN lives and writes in Montana. Her play *Elizabeth the Fourth* was produced as part of the Annual Off-Off Broadway Short Play Festival in 1993. *Something Happened Here* is published in *Play It Again!*, a collection of one-acts. Her other plays include *Doing the Laundry*, *The Patrician Potty*, and the full-length script, *Season's Greetings*. Madeleine also directs, guest lectures, teaches playwriting workshops, and serves as casting coordinator for Montana motion pictures and commercials.

SUSAN MILLER is an Obie Award-winning playwright whose works *Nasty Rumors and Final Remarks*, *For Dear Life*, and *Flux* were produced by Joseph Papp and the New York Shakespeare Company. She has also been produced by The Second Stage, The Mark Taper Forum, and Naked Angels, among others. A Eugene O'Neill playwright, she has received fellowships from the National Endowment for the Arts, a Rockefeller Grant, and has twice been a finalist for the Susan Smith Blackburn Prize in Playwriting.

PAMELA MILLS was born in Zululand and raised in Port Elizabeth, South Africa. After studying English and Drama at the University of Cape Town, she got her first professional job as a stage manager and actress with the Space Theatre Company, South Africa's first non-segregated theatre, founded by Athol Fugard, Brian Astbury, and Yvonne Bryceland. She began writing for children in 1983, and her first play, *A Matter of Time* or *The Wondrous Adventures of Starklith and Maccoboy Mole*, was performed at the Market Theatre in Johannesburg in 1985. In 1988 she came to the United States, and now lives in Cambridge, Massachusetts with her husband.

DIANNE MONROE grew up in a small southern town during the years that Jim Crow was crumbling. Later, she became part of the grass roots movement of that time. Her education began by listening to "oldheads" tell their stories on the front porches of shotgun shacks, and continued on the front stoops of urban inner-city wastelands. It was out of this soil that her first play, *Alabama Red Dirt*, was born. Ms. Monroe's short stories and articles have been published in both literary magazines and commercial periodicals. She is currently developing several other scripts.

CHERRIE MORAGA is a poet, playwright, and essayist. She is the co-editor of *This Bridge Called My Back: Writings by Radical Women of Color* which won the Before Columbus American Book Award in 1986. She is the author of numerous plays including *Shadow of a Man*, winner of the 1990 Fund for New American Plays Award, and *Heroes and Saints*, winner of the Will Glickman Prize in 1992. Her most recent book is a collection of poems and essays entitled *The Last Generation*. Ms. Moraga is also a recipient of the National Endowment for the Arts' Theatre Playwrights Fellowship. *Giving Up the Ghost* appears in *Heroes and Saints and Other Plays*, published by West End Press, Albuquerque, NM, 1993.

LAVONNE MUELLER is currently director of Playwriting at the University of Iowa. Her plays include *Killings on the Last Line, Little Victories, The Only Woman General, Colette in Love, Crimes and Dreams, Breaking the Prairie Wolf Code, The Assassination of Federico Garcia Lorca, Letters to a Daughter from Prison, Violent Peace*, and *Five in the Killing Zone*. Her work has been produced in regional theatres and in New York at the American Place Theatre, Theatre Four, Apple Corps Theatre, Samuel Beckett Theatre, Horace Mann Theatre, and Nat Horne Theatre. *Letters to a Daughter* toured India, and *The Only Woman General* was "Pick of the Fringe" at the Edinburgh Festival. She has held Woodrow Wilson Visiting Scholar, Fulbright, NEA, NY Foundation for the Arts, NEH, Illinois Arts Council, Guggenheim, and Rockefeller grants.

JANET NEIPRIS' plays include *Statues, Exhibition, The Bridge at Belharbour, The Agreement* (PBS Radio, "Earplay," Best Short Plays of 1987), *The Desert* (PBS Radio, "Earplay"), *Separations, Out of Order, Almost in Vegas, Notes on a Life, 703 Walk Hill, Brussels Sprouts (Kenyon Review),* and *A Small Delegation* (W. Alton Jones Award, 1992). Her work has been produced at major regional theatres including the Arena Stage, The Goodman, Center Stage, Philadelphia Festival Theatre, Milwaukee Rep, and in New York at Circle Rep, The Women's Project, and The Manhattan Theatre Club. She also writes for film and television. Ms. Neipris has received a Schubert Fellowship, an NEA Playwriting grant, and a Rockefeller Foundation Fellowship.

JANET OVERMYER is an Instructor in the Department of English at Ohio State University. She has published fiction, nonfiction (scholarly and personal essays), poems, and book reviews. Her plays include *We Only Meet at Funerals, Stories Women Tell,* and three linked short plays: *A Staircase Named Desire, Double Staircase,* and *The Staircase Knows.* Her plays have been performed in Columbus as well as off-off-Broadway. She is owned by Dana, Caitlin, Molly, and Ashley, the four most beautiful cats in Columbus. "Emily" comes from a longer piece, *Emily Through the Years.*

KATY PETTY was born on the Taurus-Gemini cusp. She wrote the monologue *Pocket* in 1992 to perform in the American College Theatre Festival's Irene Ryan Competition for actors. It proved a winner and she went on to the finals at the Kennedy Center in Washington, DC. Her latest works include the plays *Unsung, Aquaphile* and *Unslung Hero.* Her favorite color is audacious red.

ANNE PHELAN has been playwright-in-residence at Chelsea Rep and the Perishable Theatre, and is currently a member of the Writers Unit of the Aboutface Theatre Company. Her plays (*Romance Play, L., The Second Mrs. Wilson, White Gloves, Wake: A Farce, Thomas Dorr*, and *The Sixth Age*) have been produced off-off-Broadway, in Rhode Island and Massachusetts, and on PBS station WSBE. She has been a semi-finalist in many playwriting contests, including Village Gate, Philadelphia Theatre Company, and Writer's Digest, and is also a member of the Dramatists Guild.

SHARON HOUCK ROSS has served as playwright-in-residence at The Women's Project & Productions in New York City, where she began and coordinated the Playwrights' Lab. Her plays have been produced widely and carried on National Public Radio. Most recently, *Trapped Daylight*, an exploration of the mythic roots of domestic violence, was produced off-off-Broadway; *Game*, a one-woman show, was produced by Circle Rep's Lab Theatre; and *A Melting Season*, concerning two Cayuse Indian women's spiritual quests, received a reading at The Women's Project.

TAMMY RYAN received an M.F.A. in Playwriting from Carnegie-Mellon University in 1990, and a Pennsylvania Council on the Arts Playwriting Fellowship for 1991–1992. "Stupid People" and "Ashes, Ashes" are excerpted from her monologue play, *Souls on Board*, which has been performed across the United States. Her other works include *Pig, Deadman Walking, Flying Pigeons, Closed in Places*, and *The Boundary*. She teaches at Point Park College in Pittsburgh, where she lives with her husband and their daughter.

ELISABETH SAMPSON is a graduate of the University of Massachusetts at Amherst, where she received her bachelor's degree in English and Theatre. In addition to her writing, Elisabeth enjoys designing and hooking up theatre lights, as well as theatre management, and teaching drama, crafts, and AIDS education at a Boys and Girls Club.

JUDY SHEEHAN is a founding member of the comedy group Artificial Intelligence. Together, the company wrote and performed many shows, including the long-running hit *Tony 'n Tina's Wedding*. Her plays *Women 101, See Jane Run,* and *Baby, It's Cold Outside* have been performed in New York, Los Angeles, Portland, and Ann Arbor. *See Jane Run* is currently being filmed by Frank Kosempi. *Bright Girls, Stupid Lives* has received staged readings at Stamford TheatreWorks, Hilberry Theatre, and Nebraska Rep. Her work as a translator includes translations of Genet and Ionesco. Judy is the tenth of twelve children and, therefore, favors ensemble work.

AMY SILBERMAN received her B.F.A. from Emerson College, where her first play, *Dry Your Eyes, Ruby Tuesday,* was produced in 1985. In 1987, Harvard University produced *Silent Sins,* a play about domestic violence which she co-wrote with Laureen Smith. Ms. Silberman's latest play, *Buying Rilke for the Paperboys,* was presented at the Paradise Rock Club in 1992 as a benefit for the AIDS Action Committee. Ms. Silberman's poetry and freelance music reviews have been published regionally, and she is currently at work on a novel. When not writing, Ms. Silberman is an Executive Assistant for International Data Group in Boston.

STEPHANIE SIMPSON, born in Shawnee, Oklahoma, grew up in various small Oklahoma towns. She graduated from Yale with a double major in Russian and Theatre Studies. At Yale, she wrote and directed her first play, *Why the Cricket Hides.* She was a Presidential Scholar in the Arts, and a finalist in the National Arts Recognition and Talent Search in both acting and writing. She recently completed the acting programs at A.R.T.'s Institute for Advanced Theatre Training at Harvard. *Equal Unto the Angels* was given a staged reading at the A.R.T. Institute and at the Intersection of the Arts in San Francisco.

DONNA SPECTOR has had eight of her plays produced off-Broadway, off-off-Broadway, regionally, and in Canada. In 1985, *Another Paradise* was given an Equity Showcase by the Open Space Theatre Experiment in New York, and in 1986 the play was produced at the Players Theatre. In 1990, Ms. Spector received a National Endowment for the Humanities grant to research the women in Greek tragedies in Greece, and she has recently received a grant from the Geraldine Dodge Foundation to produce her play *Not for the Ferryman*. She teaches fiction and playwriting at the Summer Arts Institute at Rutgers University.

CARIDAD SVICH, a playwright and translator of Cuban, Croatian, Argentine, and Spanish descent, was born in Philadelphia and now lives in Los Angeles. She recently completed four years as playwright-in-residence at INTAR, where she trained with Maria Irene Fornes. Her plays include *Gleaning/Rebusca* (produced by Beyond Baroque Literary/Arts Center in Venice, CA), *But There Are Fires* (at The Women's Project in New York), and *Any Place But Here* (produced by INTAR and Latino Chicago Theatre). Her translations include Victor Manuel Leites' *Dona Ramona*, Antonio Buero Vallejo's *The Story of a Staircase*, and Lorca's *Chimera* and *Love of Don Perlimplin*.

PAULA VOGEL is a playwright, screenwriter, and professor. She has headed Brown's Playwriting Workshop since 1985. She has also taught a theatre workshop for women in maximum security at the Adult Corrections Institute in Rhode Island. Her play *The Baltimore Waltz* premiered at New York's Circle Rep Theatre, directed by Anne Bogart. It garnered an Obie for Best Play, 1992, and received the AT&T New Play Award. *And Baby Makes Seven* was produced by Circle Rep in 1993, directed by Calvin Skaggs. *The Oldest Profession* has had several stage productions and is currently optioned for a film.

Desdemona was co-produced at Bay Street Theatre Festival and then moved to Circle Rep in 1993. *Hot 'n' Throbbing* will be directed by Anne Bogart at the American Repertory Theatre in 1994. She is currently working on a full-length play concerning Farinelli, the eighteenth-century castrato singer.

NAOMI WALLACE is a poet and playwright. She has recently had plays produced at London's Finborough Theatre (*The War Boys*), The London New Play Festival (*In the Fields of Aceldama*), and the University of Iowa (*In the Heart of America*). She has been published in the U.K. and the United States, and broadcast on B.B.C. Radio. Her first book of poems is forthcoming from Peterloo Poets Press (U.K.). *The Fish Story* was first directed by Pauline Tyler at the University of Iowa in 1993.

ROSE WEAVER is an actress, singer, and playwright. She spent eleven years, from 1973 to 1984, as a resident member of the Trinity Repertory Company in Providence, RI. During this time, she also wrote and produced *Another Christmas Miracle*, which was nominated for five New England Emmys and has been broadcast every Christmas since on WJAR-TV. She recently returned to Providence after six years in Los Angeles, where she tackled many stage and screen roles, as well as developing her unique jazz and blues style with Conrad Janis and the Beverly Hills Unlisted Jazz Band.

MARJORIE ZOHN is an actress and director with Shakespeare & Company in Lenox, MA. For the past two summers, she has directed Shakespeare & Young Company, a training and apprenticeship program for students aged 15–19. In 1991, Ms. Zohn co-wrote *Nantucket Masters*, a play commissioned by Actors Theatre of Nantucket. She also authored several short theatre pieces which were staged at Brown University.

Performance Rights

Professionals and amateurs are hereby warned that the monologues in this volume, being fully protected under the copyright laws of the United States of America, the British Empire, including the Dominion of Canada, and all other countries of the copyright union, are subject to royalty. All rights, including professional, amateur, motion picture, recitation, lecturing, public reading, radio and television broadcasting, and the rights of translation into foreign languages are strictly reserved. Particular emphasis is placed on the matter of readings and all uses of the plays by educational institutions, permission for which must be secured from the authors or their agents, as listed below:

Nancy Bagshaw-Reasoner, c/o Victoria Eide, Creative Casting, Inc., 860 Lumber Exchange Building, 10 South 5th Street, Minneapolis, MN 55402. Deborah Baley, c/o Brevoort Residence, 1007 B Long Beach Blvd., North Beach, NJ 08008. Sallie Bingham, c/o Heinemann, 361 Hanover Street, Portsmouth, NH 03801-3912. Elsie Ervin Bock, c/o Heinemann, 361 Hanover Street, Portsmouth, NH 03801. Beth Browde, c/o Ann Rittenberg Literary Agency, 14 Montgomery Place, Brooklyn, NY 11215. Heidi Carla, c/o Heinemann, 361 Hanover Street, Portsmouth, NH 03801. Bridget Carpenter, c/o Heinemann, 361 Hanover Street, Portsmouth, NH 03801. Pearl Cleage, c/o Howard Rosenstone, Rosenstone and Wender, 3 East 48th Street, 4th Floor, New York, NY 10017. Alice Eve Cohen, c/o Barbara Hogenson, Lucy Kroll Agency, 390 West End Avenue, New York, NY 10024. Karen Cronacher, c/o Heinemann, 361 Hanover Street, Portsmouth, NH 03801. Edwidge Danticat, c/o Heinemann, 361 Hanover Street, Portsmouth, NH 03801. Eve Ensler, c/o Carol Bodie, C.A.A., 9830 Wilshire Blvd., Beverly Hills, CA 90212. Kathleen Germann, c/o Heinemann, 361 Hanover Street, Portsmouth, NH 03801. Jolene Goldenthal, c/o Helen Merrill Agency, 435 West 23rd Street, New York, NY 10011. Jane Hill, c/o Heinemann, 361 Hanover Street, Portsmouth, NH 03801. Tina Howe, c/o Flora Roberts, Inc., 157 West 57th Street, New York, NY 10019. Samantha Grace Kelly, c/o Heinemann, 361 Hanover Street, Portsmouth, NH 03801. Sherry Kramer, c/o Michael Traum, Dun Buchwald, 10 East 44th Street,

New York, NY 10017. Sarah Jane Lapp, c/o Heinemann, 361 Hanover Street, Portsmouth, NH 03801. Joan Lipkin, c/o Heinemann, 361 Hanover Street, Portsmouth, NH 03801. Florencia Lozano, c/o Heinemann, 361 Hanover Street, Portsmouth, NH 03801. Michel Magee, c/o Heinemann, 361 Hanover Street, Portsmouth, NH 03801. Madeleine Martin, 2936 Millice Avenue, Billings, MT 59102-6642. Susan Miller, c/o Joyce Ketay Agency, 1501 Broadway, Suite 1910, New York, NY 10036. Pamela Mills, c/o Heinemann, 361 Hanover Street, Portsmouth, NH 03801. Dianne Monroe, c/o Heinemann, 361 Hanover Street, Portsmouth, NH 03801. Cherrie Moraga, c/o Heinemann, 361 Hanover Street, Portsmouth, NH 03801. Lavonne Mueller, University of Iowa, Department of Theatre, Iowa City, IA 52242. Janet Neipris, c/o Lois Berman/Judy Boals, 21 West 26th Street, New York, NY 10010. Janet Overmyer, c/o Heinemann, 361 Hanover Street, Portsmouth, NH 03801. Katy Petty, c/o Heinemann, 361 Hanover Street, Portsmouth, NH 03801. Anne Phelan, c/o Heinemann, 361 Hanover Street, Portsmouth, NH 03801. Sharon Houck Ross, c/o Heinemann, 361 Hanover Street, Portsmouth, NH 03801. Tammy Ryan, c/o Heinemann, 361 Hanover Street, Portsmouth, NH 03801. Elisabeth Sampson, c/o Heinemann, 361 Hanover Street, Portsmouth, NH 03801. Judy Sheehan, c/o Heinemann, 361 Hanover Street, Portsmouth, NH 03801. Amy Silberman, c/o Heinemann, 361 Hanover Street, Portsmouth, NH 03801. Stephanie Simpson, c/o Heinemann, 361 Hanover Street, Portsmouth, NH 03801. Donna Spector, c/o Heinemann, 361 Hanover Street, Portsmouth, NH 03801. Caridad Svich, c/o Audrey Skirball-Kenis Theatre, 9478 West Olympic Blvd., #304, Beverly Hills, CA 90212. Paula Vogel, c/o Peter Franklin, The William Morris Agency, 1350 Avenue of the Americas, New York, NY 10019. Naomi Wallace, c/o Rod Hall, AP Watt Ltd., 20 John Street, London, WC1N 2DR, England. Rose Weaver, c/o Heinemann, 361 Hanover Street, Portsmouth, NH 03801. Marjorie Zohn, c/o Heinemann, 361 Hanover Street, Portsmouth, NH 03801.

LIVERPOOL JOHN MOORES UNIVERSITY
Aldham Robarts L.R.C.
TEL. 051 231 3701/3634